How Does Life
Speak to Us?
Ayşe ALTUNKOPRU

Ayse Altunkopru

Ayse Altunkopru was born in Antalya in 1985. She graduated from the International Relations Department of Kırıkkale University. She is married and a mother of three. She practiced journalism in Istanbul for 8 years. After 4 years as a reporter, she worked as a page editor and writer on family-health-life issues. She left her country in 2016. With her professional success, she obtained the Extraordinary Ability Green Card (EB1), also known as the Einstein visa, and settled in America. She received training in Life Coaching, Holistic Living, Ilm-i Sima, Feng Shui, Zen Energy and Meditation, Inner Teaching Workshop, Spiritual Information and Spiritualism, Family and Relationship Constellations, Somatic Experiencing, ICF Life Coaching, Family Models, Space Energies, Symbols, Dream, and Masculine Feminine Energy. As hobbies, she practices taekwondo and she got a gold medal in 2024, knits, and has an organic garden. She currently lives in Houston and provides online individual counseling and training. She still writes about her experiences on Instagram, her account nick name is @aysescosmos.

How Does Life Speak to Us?

Ayşe ALTUNKOPRU
Translated by: Norah KOSE

HOW DOES LIFE SPEAK TO US?

Copyright © Ayse Altunopru, 2024

The copying, reproduction, use, publication, and distribution of the writings, photographs, and other contents included in this book, either partially or entirely, without permission is strictly prohibited. Legal action will be taken against those who do not comply with this prohibition. All rights reserved for this product.

ISBN

979-8-9900236-1-1

CONTENTS

INTRODUCTION 7
HOW DO DISEASES HEAL US? 10
WHAT'S YOUR PURPOSE IN LIFE? 13
WHY ARE THOSE WHO WE MEET ON THE SAME PATH OF LIFE DIFFERENT? 15
HOW DID YOU CARRY WHAT YOU COULDN'T FORGIVE? 17
DO YOU HAVE A *FORGIVENESS LIST? 19
WHO ARE YOU CUTTING OFF FROM YOUR LIFE? 22
WHO IS THAT YOU CAN'T CUT TIES WITH? 24
ARE YOU ON THE RIGHT FREQUENCY? 26
WHAT ARE YOU NOT TAKING ACTION ON? 28
WHO ARE YOU ATTRACTING INTO YOUR LIFE IN YOUR RELATIONSHIPS? 29
ARE YOU AFRAID OF AGING? 31
HAVE YOU MADE A DEAL WITH LIFE? 33
WHY IS THE WORLD UNJUST? 34
WHERE DOES SOCIAL DECAY BEGIN? 35
WHAT MAKES US WHO WE ARE? 37
WHY DOES A FRIENDSHIP END? 38
WHAT IS YOUR CONTRIBUTION TO THE WHOLE? 40
ARE YOU WILLING TO CHANGE? 42
WHY SHOULD YOU SLOW DOWN TO SPEED UP? 44
WHAT NEGATIVITY HAVE YOU TURNED INTO MOTIVATION FOR YOURSELF? 46
WHAT WOULD YOU LIKE TO CHANGE? 48
WHO CAN WE FIX? 50
HOW DOES LIFE SPEAK TO US? 51
WHAT QUESTIONS DO YOU CAST A SPELL ON YOURSELF? 53
WHY ARE POSITIVE BALANCED BY NEGATIVE? 55
ARE YOU CLICKING ON THE ROPE OF RIGHTEOUSNESS? 57
DOES HAVING HIGH FEMININE ENERGY, MAKE A WOMAN ATTRACTIVE? ... 59
WHAT ARE THE THINGS YOU ARE AFRAID TO LOSE? 61
HAVE YOU GOT OUT OF WOUNDED CHILD SYNDROME? 63
ARE YOU ATTRACTING WHAT YOU LABEL IN YOUR MIND? 64
WHAT DOES YOUR PROBLEM WITH AUTHORITY TELL YOU? 66

DOES KNOWLEDGE HEAL PEOPLE?	68
HOW DO INDIVIDUALS LEANING TOWARDS EXTREMISM BECOME MORE ENTRENCHED IN THEIR BELIEFS?	70
IN WHICH EMOTION ARE YOU EXCESSIVELY INDULGING?	73
HEY DERVISH, HOW DID YOU FIND PEACE?	75
WHO ARE THE SAVIORS?	77
WHO TAKES ON THE ROLE OF THE VICTIM?	79
WHO IS OVERLY EMPATHETIC?	82
WHY DOES THE HEART FEEL, YET THE HUMAN DOESN'T UNDERSTAND?	84
WHY DO SOME PEOPLE LIKE NEGATIVITY?	86
IS YOUR MIND STILL ON THOSE YOU LOST?	88
WHAT LEVEL IS YOUR AWARENESS?	90
CAN'T THOSE WHO CANNOT DIE IN THE PAST BE BORN INTO THE NEW?	92
WHERE DO YOU BELONG?	94
POSTPONING YOUR LIFE?	95
WAS THE PAST BETTER THAN TODAY?	97
ARE THERE ANY THINGS YOU INSIST?	99
DID YOU BUILD YOUR OWN PARADISE?	101
WALKING WHICH PATHS SEEM DAUNTING TO YOU?	103
SOUR OR SWEET?	104
DO I HAVE THE PROBLEM?	105
BUT THE PROBLEM IS NOT WITH ME, IT'S WITH THE OTHER PERSON!	107
WHAT DID YOUR BIRTH TELL YOU?	109
WHY DON'T I HAVE FRIENDS AROUND ME LIKE I USED TO?	111
IS YOUR ENERGY FLOWING IN THE RIGHT DIRECTION?	113
SOMEWHERE THERE IS A GIRL WITH A PEACH	115
DO YOU KNOW THE QUEEN OF THE NIGHT?	117
WHAT IS THE REAL MESSAGE OF SOMEONE HASSLING YOU?	119
IS HUMAN ONLY ROOTED IN THE WORLD?	121
ARE YOU SEARCHING FOR YOUR PATH?	123
WHAT IS SPIRITUAL EQUILIBRIUM?	125

INTRODUCTION

Three things accelerate a person's development in a physical, mental, or spiritual sense: illness, trauma, and the death of loved ones. For me, traumas were the things that accelerated this speed. I experienced a period in my life where I lost almost everything. My home, my belongings, my profession, my career, my friends, my homeland, my country… When I left everything behind and moved to America at the age of 30, I deeply experienced and felt what it meant to be at material and spiritual ground zero. I felt like I was in a pit. I wrote a note then: "The dust of a storm is settling over me. I feel like I've been pushed into a well, stabbed in the back. Neither real like reality nor false like lies." Yes, either that well was going to pull me even deeper, or I would know how to get out of there. Although it was difficult, I chose the second option.

I then entered an almost 4-year period of seclusion. At first, my soul withdrew to the deepest depths of my two-room house. It was a period when I questioned both myself and my faith. I knocked on many doors, received spiritual and psychological help. I started dozens of hobbies and attended language classes. While I was taking training and certificates, on the one hand, I realized the life tasks presented to me. And my soul began to climb out of that well step by step. **Where I intended to leave behind many things I thought I knew, my rigidities, my walls, the dogmas in my mind, I encountered novelties. I met life readings beyond what I knew.** There was another me inside of me. In fact, I needed every difficulty I experienced to let go of what I held on to tightly, to be flexible, and to change. Sometimes, I saw how I attracted events that knocked me down and understood that no one was to blame. I needed everything I experienced, and they had come to heal me. I made peace with my past and thanked them repeatedly for what they taught me. The divine system was not tormenting me; it was bringing me into balance with what it was making me experience. As my perspective on the past changed, my life began to change materially and spiritually. Thus, the first eight years of my journey to find myself passed with journalism, and the second eight years passed with the journey of finding myself.

Since my profession is already about writing, I started to write about what benefited me and what I realized on my Instagram account @aysescosmos. While I thought I had given up on writing, I understood that my healing increased as I wrote and shared with others. I felt my soul healing more as I wrote about what our life tasks taught us. Sometimes inspiration came at night when everyone was asleep, sometimes while I was breastfeeding my baby, sometimes while washing the dishes… As I wrote on social media, those who found something of themselves began to follow, and my account grew slowly and organically. I was very excited to find that what I wrote resonated with others. I received tremendous support from people I didn't know whose faces I hadn't seen. Because even though our lives and experiences were different, our feelings were the same. Many people, like me, were experiencing change and looking for a way out. I wasn't alone; we were pieces of a whole.

We embarked on a journey together, slowly developing our souls and opening up new topics in reading life. We started to heal together. Words fly away, but writing remains. And reading is as healing as writing. However, what is written and read in digital format is less permanent and effective than paper. With this intention, I started to collect the expanded version of my writings on my computer. Then, the idea of this book came up. I offer this book first to my soul and then to the healing of those who read it. We are still on the road together, healing together. I am on the writing side.

Many people have accompanied me on this journey, and they deserve thanks. But my most enormous thanks is to my dear husband Hanifi, who has always been by my side, always made me feel his support, lifted me up when I fell, and has been my companion and friend... I am so grateful to you. And my life teachers, my dear children Osman, Vera, and Elina, this journey would have been incomplete and tasteless without you. Your existence and motherhood completed me. When you reach adulthood and read this book, I hope you will take this journey we walked together further with the treasure of your own life, in your way, joyfully and perceptively. I love you all so much.

January 26, 2024

HOW DO DISEASES HEAL US?

I am someone who strives to progress on my journey of self-awareness and awakening. I both receive and give education on behalf of collective consciousness. There have been many topics that have changed the course of my life. One of these issues was the emergence of a tumor in my left arm. This visitor helped me refresh my perspective on life and myself. The left side represents the past, and the tumor was right on the heart meridian on the left side. Moreover, I was in a period where I had not yet done a liver and gallbladder detox, and I intended to release the accumulated anger and rigidity in these areas. This visitor that emerged on top of the feelings I experienced in those days also revealed the burdens in my heart. In fact, when the feelings inside me came to the surface, it also revealed itself. Well, when you intend for your soul to heal, the body supports in this way.

Through tests and ultrasounds, we were given another surprise from Allah during the same period. I was pregnant. The doctor postponed my farewell to the visitor in my arm to after childbirth. However, this time I was going through a process different from my other pregnancies. I had even forgotten about my arm. My stomach didn't accept anything I ate, including water. I was even removing the bile fluids from my stomach on an empty stomach. I couldn't leave the house for 3 months. It was a tremendous cleansing process. The baby said, "It's very complicated here, Mom, you need to clean up," I think, and he cleaned me up. I confronted my accumulated, hidden emotional residues, that is, my escapades. It was hard.

I came to my senses a bit, and the landlord said he was going to sell the house. As if to say, "Now you've entered a cleansing process, say goodbye to the old.". Our process of finding a new home and moving began. The market had risen in America, and finding a house had become quite difficult. We made offers on many houses, but none were accepted. Then we suddenly found a house that suited us. But now the process of moving was beginning. And my feeling was that I needed to cleanse myself of the burdens and excesses in the old house. I sold most of my belongings. I got rid of excesses, old things, and the past, and then I moved. Pregnant, I slowly settled in with my own hands. This was another cleansing process I experienced during the same period. And I said 'hello' to the new and the novelties.

In short, that year taught me a serious lesson. I didn't even share this process with most of my closest friends. I didn't ask for help from anyone. Because I thought I needed to turn inward and experience my awareness thoroughly. Some took offense when I cut off the relationship. However, considering our conditions, I thought I was the one who should be asked about my well-being. But I had no expectations from anyone. I am still in a point in my life where I say 'welcome' with love to those who come and 'goodbye' with love to those who go. I am in a state of effortless letting go. I do not violate the boundaries I drew for the sake of courtesy and respect, and I say "no" as much as I can.

I now look at the world differently. But I still have a distance from those who continue to hurt my heart. Because I have also realized the value of my heart. Our human feelings are also entrusted, just like our bodies. Accumulating causes pain in healing as well. Unexpressed heartaches invite visitor illnesses to the body. Illnesses come to heal us, to see ourselves.

That's why spending your energy in the right place with the right people should be like a monument for humans. Because wasting that energy is also crossing your own right...

WHAT'S YOUR PURPOSE IN LIFE?

Self-awareness is a difficult task. Many people often ask themselves: What is my purpose? What do I want from this life?

Apart from being a servant to Allah, every person has a duty, a purpose in this world, and it is not the same for everyone. When a person does that job, they feel the joy of life, love life, and feel satisfied. They experience happiness and peace. Some are marble artisans who love their work, some are CEOs in a company. In fact, the difference and the reason are not only luck and opportunities. Preferences also come into play. You can be mistaken if you judge based on appearances whether someone's heart is pleased or not.

Those who cannot find the purpose and goal of their life, even if they are a sultan in a palace, live restlessly, not enjoying the moment, and constantly make their surroundings restless. Because of this restlessness, they are in motion and involve others in this restlessness. They even blame those closest to them or the authorities for what they could not achieve. However, this state of mind adds unhappiness to their unhappiness.

A person's eagerness to strive for something, being obsessed with someone, constantly wanting to go out, wanting to shop constantly even though they don't need to, addictions, etc... The common cause of all these is to be in search.

The peace one is looking for is where they are running away from, in their own center. Those who want to find their purpose in life should follow their feelings instead of running away from themselves. They should think in silence and ask themselves these questions: What makes me happy? What do

I see as obstacles in front of me? Are they really obstacles? Or did I create those obstacles? Am I the obstacle I see in front of me?

The right questions bring the right answers quickly. Before you know it, those who have become a burden, both materially and spiritually, will have become tenants for free. Then start letting go of those burdens one by one.

And sometimes there is no specific solution. There is a state of acceptance and letting go. Situations that seem uncertain or blocked in front of us test our surrender. When we leave it to the divine system, everything will fall into place on its own.

WHY ARE THOSE WHO WE MEET ON THE SAME PATH OF LIFE DIFFERENT?

Sometimes, life's path flows easier for one person, while the same path is more bumpy for another. Within the same life circumstances, one person progresses easily, while another faces difficulties in the same matter. One may knock on ten doors for a job, and none open, while another earns money at the second door. One gets married, and life becomes easier, while another's life becomes harder after marriage.

Those who take the easy path may disturb the other. The one struggling may compare themselves to the other and secretly wish for them to struggle too. We can't say everyone is ill-intentioned in this regard. In fact, humans are very understanding. Because the one in a good situation cannot understand the other. The one struggling wants to be understood, and beyond that, they want to understand why things are the way they are. Life seems unfair to humans because of this. But the divine system's understanding of justice does not work as humans know it. The scales of life's justice work more delicately than we think. What matters there is balance regarding the issues you see and do not see.

Some people always look at what they don not have and envy them, but they fail to realize that they don not need the things they don not have. That's why different doors open for all of us on the same path. Because our life tasks and needs are different. The other person's test comes from different issues, from a place you do not see. You may not see it, but he will experience his own test when the time comes.

Therefore, instead of looking at the other's life that you think is easy, understand your own duty. Your healing is there.. What is little for you may be as much as you need. There is another place to spend your trapped energy. Do your homework first, realize that, that trouble brings you into balance, and complete your homework.

Then ask yourself the right question: Am I done needing this trouble? The answer you give will open a new tab in your fate scene...

HOW DID YOU CARRY WHAT YOU COULDN'T FORGIVE?

Is there anyone among us who is not upset with anyone? I think there aren't many. Because people evolve with each other. Disappointments teach us a lot in life.

Forgiveness/reconciliation is not a final point reached. It is sometimes an inner struggle that lasts a lifetime. Forgiving someone, making an inner reconciliation, does not mean taking them back into your life. On the contrary, it is better to stay away from those who do not bring you positive energy. After our Prophet (peace be upon him) said that he forgave Hz. Wahshi, who killed his beloved uncle Hz. Hamza, he said: "When I see you, I remember my uncle and I am sad." That's why he makes it clear that he does not want to meet him face to face and after that day, Hz. Wahshi does not appear to our Prophet until he dies. He stands behind the columns in prayers.

Maybe we have not experienced such difficult reconciliations, but ultimately what is difficult for a person is relative. These days, it is very easy to say "forgive." It is also not easy to forgive someone who has hurt you deeply, say, "He made me suffer a lot, but this painful experience taught me a lot" and forgive immediately, pretending as if nothing had happened. Leaving aside our humane and mortal side requires serious maturity.

However, the process of forgiveness/reconciliation is a very beautiful experience and experiment that makes a great progress for evolution. It is actually getting rid of a heavy burden that one puts on their own shoulders. Especially, grudge, hatred, and anger are heavier burdens that pull a person down and down, rather than coming from the other side. Living with these burdens makes life very short. While the beauties of the world, which we are allowed to experience, pass by, there is no benefit for a person to constantly anchor to the past.

If loving the created for the sake of the Creator is the goal, let us strive and intend to extinguish the fires in our hearts for His sake. The rest will come easily.

DO YOU HAVE A *FORGIVENESS LIST?

Every soul that comes to experience worldly life, as part of its evolution, sometimes stumbles, sometimes loses, sometimes gets hurt, and sometimes hurts others. Do you think that a person needs to be hurt and to hurt others? Yes, they do.

The problems a person experiences with their surroundings develop, change, transform, and grow that person. This is how we complete each other. However, those who do not understand their mistakes, who do not see the lesson life is giving them, continue to experience the same negative experiences repeatedly because they have not completed their assignment. They also enter into the energy of cause and effect, known as karma.

Without forgiveness, without pardoning, without reconciliation, a person cannot advance their evolution of the soul. Because they get stuck somewhere in the past. Since they continue in that energy, they attract similar experiences into their lives. Instead of soaring through levels of the soul, they get stuck in a vicious cycle. They tie the world and the world's coarse emotions to their feet. They feed on the negative and cannot progress.

What I have noticed about myself is this: Almost all of my minor resentments that have weighed me down have been things I did not express, but rather expected the other party to understand. I withdrew, acted cold, and cut off the relationship, expecting the other party to understand their mistake, the point where they hurt and upset me. Unfortunately, in the face of the harshness of the world, this is a behavior that is too subtle. It is so subtle that most people cannot see it. And of course, in the face of this incomprehensible coldness, the other party distances themselves.

Without reconciliation, there are irreversible separations. In most disputes, it is not fully known why someone is upset and what they are upset about. Everyone writes their own story from their own perspective. And unresolved issues and gossip remain.

That's why resentments and hurt feelings need to be expressed in a timely manner. It doesn't matter whether the other party agrees with you or not. What matters is expressing yourself. What will heal you is not the other party agreeing with you. What's important is to timely pour water on the fire that has the potential to grow within you and to express this to the other party. Perhaps you will find a necessary explanation. Of course, the skill is in being able to do this without hurting or offending. Engaging in a fight only amplifies negative energy and fulfills the opposite intention. The aim is to open the door to reconciliation.

My advice is this: Make a list of forgiveness for yourself from the past to the present. There are certainly those you couldn't talk to one-on-one, those you couldn't reconcile with, or those you don't have the opportunity to reconcile with. When you feel ready and comfortable, talk to them one by one internally. Imagine inviting them to a table, around a campfire, or to any environment you desire, offer them tea or coffee. Then talk to them, pour out your feelings, cry and release your emotions if you need to. Then forgive them, leave the burdens there. You can even write it on paper and burn it. Human beings are high-frequency energy. And the other person's soul feels your energy. Those who can do these face-to-face will achieve greater benefit and healing. But the technique

I am talking about is not about the other party's feelings. It is about your relief and emotional healing.

Let's remember; if all these feelings like being hurt and hurting others are managed correctly, they enlarge the soul and benefit its evolution. After all, people evolve with each other.

* We used forgiveness in the place of Helalleşmek. "Helalleşmek" is a Turkish word that does not have a direct equivalent in English. It refers to the act of making amends, settling a dispute, or seeking forgiveness and reconciliation, often in a spiritual or moral context. It involves both parties agreeing to forgive and move on from past grievances.

WHO ARE YOU CUTTING OFF FROM YOUR LIFE?

Do you have people you want to avoid but still mention their names, gossip about, and dream about? Know that the connection with them continues. And cutting ties is not an easy action. This connection is not severed by simply distancing yourself. From afar, the negative energy continues with unseen wires.

So why can't a person cut ties with those they know are harming them?

What keeps these toxic ties unbroken is anger. Anger is a high-frequency energy. Behind anger lies the feeling of being right. And people often cannot cut ties because of their addiction to being right. Although they may say, "I have entrusted it to divine justice," deep down, they want to hear that they are right, to be validated in the matter that hurts them.

Trying to improve what others think of us, trying to make them know we are right, is like a disease. This desire to be right turns into an addiction, and toxic relationships continue because of it. It even replaces validation with self-proving. Feelings like 'Look, I am actually a good person, I am not like they describe me' dominate. And one starts to give a lot, sacrificing and compromising oneself. Of course, this exhausts a person both materially and spiritually.

One wants to let go, distance oneself, cut ties, but due to unresolved issues, the spiritual relationship continues. This is one of the biggest handicaps of a person and one of the situations where they harm themselves. They always want to be known as good and become addicted to hearing sentences like

"You were right, you were the one who told the truth, you are a good person."

However, the only approval that satisfies a person's soul is self-approval. After a point, those who can let go, accept what is, without forcing relationships, without feeling the need to explain themselves to others, can establish healthy ties. Divine help and the energy of the universe are with them.

So let go, let others think whatever they want about you. What matters is what you think about yourself. Do you approve of yourself? Are you at peace with yourself? If this is negative, then leave the outside and work on improving the image within yourself. Because the whole secret is here. If you approve of yourself and accept yourself in every aspect, the outside world will accept and approve of you too...

WHO IS THAT YOU CAN'T CUT TIES WITH?

Do you have people you want to stay away from, but you still mention their names, gossip about them, and dream about them? Know that your connection with them continues. And cutting ties is not an easy action. This connection is not severed by simply distancing yourself. From afar, the negative energy continues with unseen threads.

So even if a person tries to cut ties with those they know harm them, why can't they do it?

What keeps these toxic ties from being cut is anger. Anger is a high-frequency energy. Behind anger lies a sense of being right. And it is mostly due to the addiction to being right that a person cannot cut ties. Even though they may say, "I have left it to divine justice," deep down, they want to hear that they are right, they want to be validated in the matter that hurts them.

Trying to improve what others think about us, trying to make them know that we are right, is like a disease. This desire to be right turns into an addiction, and toxic relationships continue because of it. It even turns from seeking validation into proving oneself. Feelings like 'Look, I am actually a good person, I am not as they describe' start to control a person. And they start to be very giving, sacrificing themselves and making concessions. Of course, this also exhausts a person materially and spiritually.

One desires to let go, to distance oneself, to cut ties, yet the unfinished business keeps the spiritual relationship alive.

This is one of the biggest handicaps of a person and one of the situations where they harm themselves. They always want to be known as good and become addicted to hearing sentences like "You were right, you were the one telling the truth, you are a good person."

Yet, the only approval that satisfies a person's soul is the approval of oneself. After a point, those who let go, accept what is, without forcing relationships, without feeling the need to explain themselves to others, can establish healthy connections. Divine help and the energy of the universe accompany them.

So let it be, let others think whatever they want about you. What matters is, what do you think about yourself? Do you approve of yourself? Are you at peace with yourself? If it's negative here, then leave the outside, and work on fixing the image in yourself. Because the whole secret is here. If you approve of yourself and accept yourself in every way, the outside will accept and approve of you too...

ARE YOU ON THE RIGHT FREQUENCY?

If we want both a healthy and energetic life, as well as a life filled with comprehension and awareness, we need to keep our own frequency and vibration high. But how?

Firstly, increasing the frequency and vibration of our body is something we do with our own efforts. No one will wave a magic wand over us. We can take advice, but at the end of the day, it is us who will improve ourselves with the strength given to each of us by the Creator and our own determination.

For this, first, doing things according to your faith, such as meditation, contemplation, remembrance, worship, increases your vibration. But these should be done consciously, not as activities. Our Prophet did not say in vain, "An hour of contemplation is sometimes more beneficial than a year of worship."

Secondly, life experiences keep our body and consciousness alive. Although the traumatic events we experience leave painful traces in our lives, they give us feelings such as survival, struggling, knowing our own worth, and connecting with our soul and higher self. To the soul that wants to escape; it reminds of its body, the world, and its duties. It adjusts the frequency settings.

Thirdly, it is the state of acceptance. Whatever has been experienced, caused pain, given pleasure, or not; truly accepting oneself and what is happening soothes the soul. The most peaceful and high-vibration person is the one who can say, "Whatever happened or is happening, it was necessary and for my good."

Lastly, being able to say "I have it too." The life we lead is our mirror. Whatever we judge, complain about, envy, dislike, or sneer at, carries a trace of us. In fact, in everyone and every event we encounter, we see a reflection of our own pieces. The day we realize and accept this, there will be no topic left to complain about or gossip about. Because the fact that what we see is our own mirror will hit us in the face.

Similarly, what we see as good and beautiful is also our mirror. When we understand this, our self-confidence will be restored, and we will understand our true value. And all of this will regulate our vibrations and frequencies, offering us a healthy and energetic life.

WHAT ARE YOU NOT TAKING ACTION ON?

Do you have a topic you want to start but just can't seem to get moving on?

If you say 'Yes,' know that you have an unfinished issue from the past in your mind. This could be related to your work life, your personal life, or your spiritual world. In any case, those who want to start something should first finish any unfinished business they have.

Let's look at the issue through the principles of energy. Starting something is yang energy. Finishing something is yin energy. And although yang energy may seem stronger in many cases, yin energy is actually stronger. So, it is harder to finish something than to start it.

That's why many people's lives are full of unfinished tasks, unfinished relationships, and unfinished emotions. Therefore, instead of making new beginnings, it is actually harder to finish what you have started. And those who cannot start something new cannot set sail for the new because they have not been able to finish what they started in the past. Then they get into a vicious cycle.

In short, if you still have things you haven't started or can't start, the question you need to ask is not "Why can't I start?" but rather "What can't I finish?"

And when a person starts asking themselves the right questions, they also find the right answers with the help of the universe and initiate the energy of completion.

Intend to finish what's unfinished and put effort into it, for God is the helper of those who start anew.

WHO ARE YOU ATTRACTING INTO YOUR LIFE IN YOUR RELATIONSHIPS?

In friendships and relationships, we generally meet with our opposites. People with different tastes and perspectives appeal to us more. Because we are interested in people who complement us in different ways or whom we complete. The choice of a spouse is also like the choice of a friend.

We tend to repel those who are the same as us. But the handicap of human beings is that in their relationships, they try to make the other person similar to themselves after a while. Sometimes, they become addicted to this futile effort. If the other person is similar, they believe that all the troubles and conflicts will end. Similarity brings harmony, but being exactly the same suffocates and begins to push away the person.

Therefore, especially friendships that start to become similar, rather than resembling each other, end over time. Although it is thought otherwise, similar tastes kill the excitement of the relationship after a while. And excitement begins to be sought in what is different. One of the reasons for this is imitation. Wearing the same clothes, speaking, mimicking, decorating, and style begin to bore the person. Because there is uniqueness in our essence. When some things are unique to us, we feel good.

In relationships, we feel safer with people whose character and interests are different. We have opened up a relationship area where we can tell about our weak and dark sides and also about the strong and different aspects of ourselves.

We have an instinct to tell and teach others things about ourselves that they do not know. This makes us feel good and confident. Or we want to learn new things beyond what we know. People who constantly talk about the same things as us, hang out in the same area of interest, start imitating us, or admire us eventually become repellent. This can lead to distancing ourselves from those around us, even with the excuse of a match.

When we discover these light and dark dynamics within ourselves, we use our willpower to decide the extent and nature of our relationships. This helps us attract healthy and long-lasting relationships into our lives.

Is it easy? No. But one of the life goals of human beings is to work on their personal and spiritual development.

ARE YOU AFRAID OF AGING?

In today's world, aging is perceived as a weakness. People fear white hair. However, white hair is a herald of mental dynamism.

Black is yin, a feminine color. It encompasses and accumulates knowledge. That's why hair is black in youth. The brain is in the process of gathering information and is youthful.

White, on the other hand, is yang, a masculine color. It reflects and disperses. It is generous. White hair heralds the time to express the knowledge accumulated in youth. Youthfulness is over, wisdom has begun. Therefore, every white hair is actually a sign of experience.

While old age may be the retirement period of the body, it is the wisdom period of the mind. It is the age where correct decisions are made after lessons learned from mistakes. Contrary to what is known, these are the times when life is truly enjoyed.

However, human beings generally spend their old age waiting for death and suffering from illness, as if they have sifted the flour and hung up the sieve of life. That's why they invite illnesses into their lives, as if it were fate. Life, fate, and old age are all a pen in our hands. We will meet with what we write and how we write it.

If you magnify aging in your mind and constantly try to delay it under the influence of popular culture, you will not benefit from the experience and wisdom of the past. You will behave inappropriately where you should behave maturely. One should own their time and live it in the best way possible.

Aging gracefully is in one's hands. Don't fear your white hair, fear the life lessons that your black hair couldn't grasp and learn. Those who fail to take this lesson and cannot accept their own time age aggressively. They narrow their own soul and also narrow the young people around them. Because their soul is unhappy. Because they couldn't read life correctly. Because instead of focusing on their own center, they spent their time in the lives of others.

HAVE YOU MADE A DEAL WITH LIFE?

Do you have any life agreements you made with life?

Have you made promises to someone in the past?

Have you given yourself tasks like "I will never leave you, I will always be by your side, I will always have your back, I will handle everything"?

Could it be that many of the ties you can't cut now are based on these unbroken agreements? Promises and agreements made with such words can sometimes even prevent a person from leaving this world comfortably. For example, could the reason why someone in a coma cannot leave this world be the verbal agreements they made with someone and couldn't break?

People create the strongest bonds when they feel insecure. They make the biggest life and verbal agreements at those times. The desire to be there for the strong person also stems from this. They want to feel safe. Later, they become dependent on this bond. When they want to leave, they can't seem to move away from there as if their feet are tied. Even if they move away, they can't forget it. Because they are stuck in the hook of internal gratitude.

Now, take another look at what you can't cut ties with. And remember your life agreements. Who do you feel indebted to and why? Who have you promised? Do you have an agreement made on paper for a job that you haven't broken? Then it's time to terminate those agreements, time to resign from your duties.

And you know what's best? You can break and renew the agreements you make with life at any moment. You can be reborn from yourself at any moment. Because everything changes moment by moment.

WHY IS THE WORLD UNJUST?

Since I heard that saying, I've been looking at the events I encounter in a different way: the world is not a place of justice, it is a place of balance. There was a side of me that couldn't tolerate injustice. Whenever I saw an oppressed person, I would stand by their side, offer help without being asked, try to fix things, and criticize the world system. Yet, no one person can overcome injustice or establish order. This sense of inadequacy only leads a person to rebellion inwardly. Those who have this mindset cannot let go, they wear themselves out and cannot read the messages of life. Because taking sides leads to being defeated. Peace lies in neutrality.

I realized that there is actually a balance in what I saw as injustice, and I also stopped burdening myself with the experiences of others. Because the justice of the divine system established in the world does not work as we think. That is, the bad outcome we expect from the other side can be very different or may not happen at all. Because what we know as bad is a part of order and balance.

Help and intervention made without being asked can involve a person in trouble. Because every person experiences an experience according to their needs. An event that seems unjust contains many balances that we do not see. Interconnected lives and intertwined events teach us something for the betterment with a domino effect. So, you need to understand that the events you cannot change should be that way. Fighting with it is just a waste of time and energy.

When you accept it, life becomes easier, and burdens become lighter. Then, let go of your burdens on this divine ship. Because the ship is safely heading to the port despite all storms...

WHERE DOES SOCIAL DECAY BEGIN?

The part belongs to the whole. If there is corruption in a part, it affects the whole. That's why corruption should be prevented when it's small. Social disinformation is also like this. Small moral corruptions that are not considered important grow over time and become normalized. It reaches a point where we start saying, "When did we become like this?" As each of us turns a blind eye to small immoral acts, treats them as if they don't affect us, a small piece of corruption spreads to the whole. From you to your surroundings, from your surroundings to your country, from your country to the world... The divine flow progresses from atom to universe.

Whenever such a sharing is made, expressions like "yes, it happened like that, they did this to the innocent, they did that, they stole, they oppressed, and no one said anything" are used. I'm not talking about others. I'm talking about you. I'm talking about whoever is reading this. I'm talking about ourselves. You, me, them, all of us. No matter what kind of victimization you have experienced. In fact, whatever you have experienced, you probably experienced it because of your own silence and turning a blind eye. If you didn't do anything, if you supported someone or if you were in a certain energy, those there did it, you turned a blind eye, and the result affected you too. There is no point in blaming others anymore. It's time to turn to ourselves!

If you're still looking for someone to blame after reading this, I'm sorry, your consciousness cannot progress. You'll remain in a low frequency, your life assignments will become harder. And you won't understand the wars happening in the world today, why innocent people are constantly dying, who serves whom, why no one spoke up, intervened, and why it will continue to escalate. Because you're still looking for someone to blame instead of seeing your assignments.

Saying this doesn't mean the oppressor is right. God is not unaware of the script He has made you watch. Your task is to understand why you are watching this script and to see your role/task in this script. What changes the divine flow is this!

Just as corruption in a part spreads to the whole, so does a correction in one part spread to the whole. Because that piece is you. You are an important part of this world. And it is the corruption of the parts that corrupts the world. So, stop cursing others, turn to yourself! Fix the part! Otherwise, unfortunately, nothing will improve in your individual life or in the world...

WHAT MAKES US WHO WE ARE?

Is it genes, family, or social environment that shapes us? Why are we different even though we grow up in the same family or environment? What shapes our behavior? These and more questions are answered in the Netflix documentary "Babies," which I really liked.

Human capacity for morality has its foundation in our essence and is innate. Babies also come with this capacity. So, everyone is born with the same innate morality. Of course, character, genetic influences, and choices can lead to some variability.

So what happens that everyone changes later on? Research shows that the most important thing in moral development is the influence of family and environment. That is, every child's ethical and moral values change over time.

One experiment in the documentary caught my attention. 8-month-old babies are shown a puppet show. A square puppet tries to cross a ledge, and a round puppet helps it. But a triangle puppet hits and pushes the square puppet down. This scene is repeated three or four times. At the end of the show, the puppets are placed in front of the babies. And all the babies choose the round, helpful puppet.

The result of the experiment teaches us a lesson: Children are parts of a larger moral society beyond our limited environment. If we raise them with the awareness that they are part of a larger society, rather than belonging only to our narrow world, a lot will change in the world.

WHY DOES A FRIENDSHIP END?

Why does a friend with whom you once had such a great time become cold and never be the same again?

The friendships formed in the first years of school are different from the friendships that remain after school ends. Likewise, when you start a job or move to a new city or country, your first friendships usually end and are replaced by new ones. Some cannot understand the coldness or spiritual distance that intervenes. He talks about disloyalty. It is said, "We used to be good, but now we stop calling and asking."

But there is something like this. Everything you experience in life is in proportion to your needs. A new friendship and existing friendships are a need to become rooted in the city or country you live in. This is not a one-sided need, but a need for solidarity established by the meeting of mutual energy. The subsequent separation is also a need. Because energy harmony is over.

This may raise the question: "Will the one in need walk away?" Yes, it usually happens, and that's the best thing to do. In relationships that are forced and managed, or in forced meetings made for the sake of love or just to relieve loneliness, there is a negative energy that is noticed but ignored. After a while, this negative energy invites a sharp event. The internal but suppressed desire to separate, together with the vertical energy of the system, gives rise to an event that will further disrupt the relationship. And separation is spontaneous but destructive. Therefore, it is good to keep a distance in order to manage this previously noticed energy well.

Sometimes, in order to hold on to old friendships, sacrifices or assistance made in the past are mentioned. This is to hook the other person with kindness. In fact, the other person does not need that help. Seeing someone in need means not knowing the divine system. The person giving help needs that kindness himself so that he can continue the relationship with his interlocutor. These relationships always end in disappointment. Because the bond established is not healthy, its expectant energy is a bad relationship.

That's why the relationships of those who continue to look at the same place without reproaching anyone, even if they meet after two years, and then look at their own lives, are healthier. It is of no use to anyone to turn the joy of conversations in the moment into a negative situation by accounting for the past.

As lives and experiences change, people also change, their energy and needs also change. Of course, friends change too. Everyone teaches something and leaves a legacy in our lives. One should know how to let go when the time comes. Energetic permission must be given to the departed. Even though there is longing, this is good for people, it is a necessary socialization and evolution process.

WHAT IS YOUR CONTRIBUTION TO THE WHOLE?

Success without purpose seems meaningless to the soul. Whatever you do, you will be satisfied if it benefits someone else. Sometimes just making yourself happy gives satisfaction. However, this only helps people up to a certain point. Because it is in nature to contribute to the whole of the divine order.

That's why achievements that are aimlessly acquired, inflated, presented by someone else, do not benefit anyone and seem like success, do not satisfy people. Could this be the reason for substance abuse, which reaches almost 60 percent in Hollywood? A nurse makes a serious contribution to society, but someone who only makes videos of the food he eats or the clothes he wears cannot achieve the same satisfaction. That's why his soul goes to try other things after a while. You see some celebrities as charity volunteers. Because the ballooning success he has achieved does not satisfy him.

This is true not only for celebrities, but for all of us. A person knows deep down whether he contributes to himself and society. When he is not satisfied, he numbs himself with an addiction. Sometimes with substances, sometimes with phones, sometimes with shoes/bags, sometimes with social media or another addiction... Because raw souls who do not know what to do in the way of real contribution to themselves and the whole are always in a search.

Nature seeks to find itself, its essence. For this reason, kindness done to others is very good for the soul of a person. Because it contributed. Look at those standing tall. They contribute to society with their profession, stance, aid, what they say and write. This satisfaction keeps them alive and moves them forward.

So are these the only contributions? Prayers made to the world, nature and humanity apart from oneself are also very good for a person. The positive frequency you spread with your thoughts and love from where you sit right now is a great contribution to the whole. The energy of the part belongs to the whole. Therefore, talking, watching, listening and even thinking about good and positive things contributes to the whole.

We are all living parts of a great energy. Every contribution to the whole, from small to large, enlarges souls and accelerates awakening.

ARE YOU WILLING TO CHANGE?

Change scares some people. Those who do not want to let go of the old, that is, those who want the same order to continue, resist change. In fact, there is a serious ego and ego involved here. Ego owners do not feel safe when some things in their lives do not go the way they want. Because what he knows is better (!) Isn't this the root of most of the problems we experience in life?

Those who stand in the way of change do not like those who change. However, systems change, ideas change, clothing styles change, eating habits change, the world keeps changing. That's why those who resist change are the ones who gossip the most. Because they keep saying things while standing like a stone in front of flowing water. For example, he says about someone who has changed, "I also know his previous states." So, that person has experienced a change, how nice. But they prefer to look at the negative and depressing side. However, how beautiful are those who start from scratch, improve themselves and improve their quality of life.

The ego, on the other hand, prevents people from being happy with someone else's change and development with various excuses. That's why he evaluates the other person with his past, not his present. But that person has already changed and set sail for the future. Because it is impossible to stand in the way of a correct change whose time has come. But the ego doesn't want to see this. He still wants the other person to remain in his past small, weak, inadequate state. Because maybe the people he despised have walked ten times the distance he couldn't take when he had the opportunity.

If a person is the same as he was 5 years ago, he is at a loss. Because if one day is the same as another, he is in loss. If the person who cared about others rather than himself yesterday does the same today, he is standing in the way of his own change.

Change is beautiful. But how can your surroundings stay the same while you change? Those who intend to change should sometimes consider loneliness and sometimes criticism. If those around you criticize your change, this shows that you are on the right track.

Life starts over again every day. One night ends, then the morning begins again and again. Spring comes after every winter. Dried branches are blooming. In other words, people are given the opportunity to start over and change, moment by moment. It is possible to initiate your own change at any time. But if you stand in the way of change, sometimes the system changes it by force. Where you resist staying the same as before, a sudden event comes and you spontaneously become the change itself. And your life changes without your control. But this is very challenging. Instead of choosing this change, choose the easy ones. Be conscious.

Then be willing to change so that what happens will happen easily.

So remember! God is the helper of those who start over.

WHY SHOULD YOU SLOW DOWN TO SPEED UP?

If there is something in your life that you want to speed up, it means you have entered a period where you need to slow down. Let me explain what I mean using an example I experienced in the market.

I went to a supermarket in America that was always busy. While I was doing my shopping and moving forward to get in line with the grocery cart, I saw that the first two registers were crowded. But the density was less at the last cash register. I walked towards it calmly. Just as I was about to get in line, a lady quickly walked in front of me and took my turn. I smiled, but she didn't look at me anyway. So I calmly moved to the next cash register row. It turned out that the last cash register that the lady passed through was further away from the others, but it was not noticeable due to the crowd. So, if there were 6 people there, there were 3 people at the next checkout I passed through. We experienced an optical illusion. Then another officer came and opened a closed safe. He gestured to me and called me to the cash register. Thus, I was at the front of the line at a new cash register, before anyone else. And all this happened in 5-6 minutes. It was as if an unseen hand quickly pushed me forward. While I was heading towards the exit of the market with the products I bought from the cash register, the lady in front of me was still in line.

This is what it's like to slow down to speed up. That state of calm will take you faster on your path. But the excessive speed and greed you use to accelerate will hold you back. You know, when mothers go out with their children, they say "come on".

But children are cooler than mountains. He looks at the color of his toy and checks its buttons.

He examines it, he is not in a hurry. The child is actually in the flow. As we grow, our rhythm gets disrupted. Instead of adapting the child's rhythm to herself, if the mother could follow that rhythm, she would calm down on her own. How beautiful is that state of tranquility where you don't have to worry about catching up with anything.

Because otherwise, those who try to speed up slow down. Of course, I'm not saying this for those trying to catch their flight. But most of the time, when one is speeding up, one is not aware of someone else's rights. He thinks that by seeing the easy way and being alert, he will be ahead of everyone else. He thinks his life will get back on track immediately. However, he does not fully see his own life or the life of those he steps on. He lives his life without clarity, like the scenery passing quickly through the train window. And it breaks its own rhythm.

For example, knitting is very good for me when I want to speed up my life. While knitting, you go with the flow and move towards the result, one by one, patiently, stitch by stitch, without needing to speed up. Then you look back and you realize that neither the cardigans, the beanies, the dolls, nor the blankets are finished.

Bottom line; I believe that a stitch made with a calm spirit in life has a positive impact on another event.

WHAT NEGATIVITY HAVE YOU TURNED INTO MOTIVATION FOR YOURSELF?

Which type of person do you encounter most often around you? What personal situations bother you the most? Is there someone around you who constantly finds faults or do you deal with people who make you feel defeated?

In this case, the first question we should ask ourselves is: Why do I need this person?

Yes, it may sound ridiculous at first. "Why would I want such a person around me? We can say, "He is clearly doing evil to me." However, it is easy to blame someone else, but it is not a solution to the problem. Ingenuity; We learn to keep negative environmental influences away from ourselves and to meet with what is good for us...

For example, a person who constantly deals with people who put him down may have regrets. That's why someone has come to mirror the places where he oppresses himself. Some people find themselves motivated by someone who criticizes them on issues they cannot take action on. He turns that person into fuel for himself and moves towards his goal with ambition. What he is trying to prove himself to someone else may actually be the area where he needs to go but is being lazy.

Some are motivated by someone who finds fault, some by money, some by supportive words. Childhood also has a great impact, but ultimately, we all have different needs.

If you have realized this, I am giving you the second correct question: Has my need for this person to treat me like this ended?

What negativity have you turned into motivation for yourself?

When you want to say goodbye to a subject and behavior, you need to replace it with something new. Because the universe does not accept emptiness. So, if you have seen your needs, leave the unhealthy ones and put healthy ones in their place. If you have cut off harmful ties, establish beneficial ones instead.

Of course, everyone is not the same. Every person is unique. Their experiences and the messages they receive are also unique. What matters is to recognize these needs and to be able to see oneself in what they experience. That's where healing begins...

WHAT WOULD YOU LIKE TO CHANGE?

Sümbül Efendi asked his students the following question: "If you could have corrected something in the world yesterday, what would it be?" The students thought about it. Some said poverty, some said incurable diseases, some said the justice system. It came to one of his students. Sümbül Efendi asked him, "And you?" The student said, "Sir, I thought about it, but everything in the universe is so orderly and centered that I couldn't find anything to fix." Sümbül Efendi smiled and said to him, "You have reached the center. From now on, your name shall be Merkez Efendi (Master of the Center)."

We are going through turbulent times with the pandemic, wars, economic crises, climate and order changes. The world is transitioning to a different order. It is clear that there are other things coming that we do not know about. However, there is no shortage of conspiracy theories, chips, people predicting the future, rituals, people sending energy in all directions, those hoping for salvation from "yes" answers, and those relying on numbers. They make the means the goal.

Everyone's mind is very confused. However, peace is in calmness. Where there is fear and anxiety, there is negative energy. People who stray from their center cling to a reason to worry and fear. Every new change or development makes them more fearful, causing them to lose their sense of trust. Someone who loses their sense of trust cannot surrender to the divine flow. Their relationship with God deteriorates.

It should not be forgotten that there is a cause above the causes that balances good and evil. He is the owner of both good and evil. Is Allah unaware of all these things, the issues you seek remedies for, and the help you expect? Whatever He does is for our good.

So, what we would say like Merkez Efendi is: there is nothing to be corrected. Everything should be as it is supposed to be, and whatever will happen in the future should be that way. The flower blooms when its time comes, and when the time comes, it returns to the earth. Just fulfill your own duties. That's all...

WHO CAN WE FIX?

I share the books and movies I like on my Instagram account, but I no longer say sentences like "you should definitely read this book, you should definitely watch that movie, please listen to this expert" even to my closest friends. I'm not defending anyone, I'm not insistently recommending anyone, I'm not taking sides.

Because no advice or coercion is of any use to those who have no demand. No matter how much we write, no matter how fancy sentences we say... Those who do not have a desire to learn something or change within themselves will not listen, and what they read or watch will not have an impact. They just pretend. He takes the book but it stays on the shelf. He reads, but the sentences hang in the air and do not reach the soul. Because he needs this deprivation. It is not time for change.

That's why since the day I realized that I couldn't fix anyone, I don't try to force anyone to tell anything or express myself. My head is cooler than the mountains. In any case, trying to correct someone is futile and is related to the person's desire to rule. So there is negative energy there and the result is not good.

If a person has a request in their mind/language, they can correct it if the wish and understands the other party. I can only correct myself, I can give advice to those who ask, and I can only be instrumental in the path to recovery. I can explain myself to anyone who asks how I am, and those who really want to listen and add something to themselves can understand what I mean.

The rest is a futile effort. Our energy is too valuable to spend on everyone.

HOW DOES LIFE SPEAK TO US?

One day, as I was driving in traffic, I asked myself about a life lesson that made me feel bad: Why did I experience this, and what is this event telling me?

At that moment, I was waiting at a red light in the left lane. I was going to turn left at the intersection. When the light turned green, I started to turn in my lane. The driver in the right lane switched to my lane while turning, and to avoid hitting him, I took the leftmost U-turn lane. With a sudden decision, I slowed down and immediately got behind him, then found a gap and quickly switched to the right lane. These happened so instantaneously in a very short distance. I was either going to make a U-turn and go back, or make the right maneuvers to switch to the other lane. Then, in the right lane I switched to, the road suddenly opened up in front of me and I accelerated. I looked in the mirror at the car that pushed me to the other lane. It was a woman driver. She was still in the left lane and also found an opportunity to switch back to the right lane. But she was left behind. If she had paid attention to her own lane, she would have progressed and not bothered me. Although I was initially angry, she taught me something. The place I was going to was my beloved taekwondo class, the one that motivates me in life.

I told myself: If you push me from my path, you will stay behind, and I will move forward. Then I realized that the sentence I said was an answer to the question I asked at the beginning. Life had quickly responded to my question with this event, in a somewhat melancholic manner.

Sometimes what you see as an obstacle speeds you up. Maybe you had leveled yourself off, life made that obstacle a teacher for you to take action. Just be sure of the path you're on, make the right maneuvers, but don't turn back because of those who bring you down. Each difficulty taught you something and made you grow. You said goodbye to those you no longer needed. Even if you couldn't quit in a healthy way in time, life forced you to quit. That's all there is to it.

WHAT QUESTIONS DO YOU CAST A SPELL ON YOURSELF?

People constantly search for the right answers in the troubles they experience. The right answers only come from the right questions we ask. Many people do not even realize that they are casting a spell on themselves by asking the wrong questions. Especially the question "how" is a powerful question. For example, questions such as "How can people be so insensitive" or "How can such cruelty/evil happen?" are powerful questions when faced with an event witnessed. Then life may say, "Come and experience." The whole point is to be a "witness" to the event that is happening at that moment. Because the Divine system is not cruel. There are many balance and life tasks that we cannot comprehend.

Now let's give examples of correct questions. Review the questions you ask about the events in your life.

- What message is there for me in this event I witnessed?

- What does my disorganization in this matter tell me?

- In what area have I gone to extremes that I am now stagnant?

- Where have I made myself feel worthless that I feel or am made to feel worthless?

- In what area am I deceiving myself that I am attracting the energy of those who lie to me?

- Am I feeling that others are jealous of me because I am jealous?

- In what area am I stagnant that I can't find time for myself or a hobby?

- If someone doesn't like me and it bothers me, perhaps I don't like something about myself?

- How can I become rich easily, healthily, and joyfully?

- Have I truly requested change that I complain about things in my life that haven't changed?

The list could go on... Let our expressions and questions change so that our lives can improve.

WHY ARE POSITIVE BALANCED BY NEGATIVE?

The conversation with unhappy people is also unhappy. They tell unhappy stories to those around them. Some become so accustomed to this toxic mindset that it becomes their character. They focus on negative developments in their own lives rather than positive ones. They always see the empty side of the glass. If that's not enough, they follow unhappy events around them or in the world, watching such negative news and series. They are skilled at finding things to be sad about, dragging themselves down and feeding on pain and negativity. This mindset suffocates those around them, reducing their circle of friends.

Even worse, some people drag down those around them who are happy. They feel discomfort towards those who laugh, have fun, go on vacation, or spend money. They try to bring others down either by belittling them or with negative words. The most insidious are those who, while shedding tears for victims, blame others for their apparent lack of empathy. According to them, while they shed tears for the victims, others are not as sensitive as they are(!) In reality, they are just distributing their own unhappiness.

If you have someone like this in your circle, let me clarify, this is not a blame game. If there is such a person in your close circle, my intention is to make you question why you are in their energy field. Yes, this person's balance in life is disrupted, and they are experiencing a difficult life task. But why are they affecting your energy? Why are you engaging with them? What is the message of your life in this situation?

Firstly, those who go too much towards the positive are balanced by the negative. Those who see life in rosy colors meet with people who will take off those glasses.

Because the world is a material plane, and negative elements cannot be ignored. Of course, do not immerse yourself in the negative, but be a witness and be aware.

Secondly, do you feel guilty about the beautiful moments you experience? Perhaps deep down, you are also judging yourself. Or you may think that you do not deserve what you have experienced or achieved. Because of this sense of worthlessness, you have encountered someone similar who judges you instead of yourself and has brought someone who judges you into your life. And they became a mirror to you.

Thirdly, do you have a need to show the beautiful things you experience to someone and to be envied? In other words, why did you bring the person you say "envies me" into your life? Perhaps being envied satisfies you in areas where you feel or are made to feel inadequate. And that's why you are keeping the person who envies you in your life.

ARE YOU CLICKING ON THE ROPE OF RIGHTEOUSNESS?

Do you have events that often come to your mind, hurt you, and make you angry? And do you often see the people related to that event in your dreams?

Let me give you an example from myself to make it clearer. It was years ago. I used to think that the negative energy of someone who hurt me was still following me, even though we hadn't seen each other. When I embarked on a journey of self-discovery and healing, I realized that I needed to make internal peace with each of these people who burdened me in this way. Yes, I was the one who was wronged, who was hurt. They were the ones who were wrong. But why should I make peace?

According to the divine system, what we experience in this worldly life is about us. The lesson is for the other side. That event or person had been a life teacher for me. I had to say goodbye to the anger that burdened me internally when I saw that message, because it was not serving me well and was pulling me back whenever I remembered it.

I did meditation for a few nights. It was like a meditation of contemplation. I delved deep into myself. I went back to that event repeatedly. I had arguments within myself about who owed what to whom. Then, as I delved deeper, I realized that the impact of the event had ended, and it had taught me a lot, but I had clung to the thread of being right. So, it was no longer about the event or the person. I had grown resentment inside me because I was not validated on that day about being right. It turned out that I was sending negative energy along with that thread of being right, and I had also hooked onto it to prove that I was right. And I wasn't even aware of it.

Some things are very difficult for a person to admit to themselves. Those who are truly ready to heal and confront themselves can do this. It takes courage. And that's where true healing is. Sometimes, to dress a festering wound, the scab must be lifted. It hurts at first, but when the 'real' ointment is applied, it heals. Otherwise, blaming the other side is the easy way out.

This confrontation shook me; my shoulders slumped. "I'm letting go of the thread of being right, I've accepted my lesson, I forgive and release my rights, and I set them free," I said. That day, it was as if a burden had lifted off me. Later, I saw that person again in my dream. "I'm leaving now," he said and bid me farewell. I understood better that I had let go of that event and the thread of being right. I never saw him in my dream again. In fact, I had set myself free.

Letting go is like that. It's like dying before dying. You no longer look back, talk about that issue, or think about it; you've closed the doors. You've liberated yourself from that lesson.

I know it's hard, but it's possible, my friends...

DOES HAVING HIGH FEMININE ENERGY, MAKE A WOMAN ATTRACTIVE?

A woman having high feminine energy is not necessarily about having curvy lines and being stylish and attractive with her gestures and clothing. When people ask me how to increase their feminine energy, I always start by saying that not everyone needs more feminine energy; perhaps staying in touch with their masculine side serves them better.

When we talk about feminine energy, the image of a flirtatious woman often comes to mind. However, what truly makes a woman feminine is her grace and compassion. By softening her mind and inner world, she finds the right feminine energy. We can't attribute rude behavior to "masculine energy." That is a corruption of masculine energy.

Just like masculine energy, feminine energy has its positives and negatives. A woman who goes to extremes with her feminine energy tends to be passive, constantly holding back, passive, and prone to being taken advantage of. She tends to be crushed under someone else's command or pressure. Now, understand why a woman who desires excessive feminine energy may not achieve the attractiveness she seeks. It's because she's not making a genuine request.

A woman with low feminine energy may exhibit excessive behavior. She may talk incessantly, shout, expend her energy and money unnecessarily, and try to control others and exert authority over them. By disrupting her feminine energy, she also shifts towards the unhealthy aspects of masculine energy. Those who try to emphasize their femininity with what they wear actually serve their masculine energy. Because excessive revealing is a masculine energy trait. It doesn't mean covering up. Whatever you overdo, you shift towards masculine energy.

A woman with healthy feminine energy is balanced. She knows when to speak up and when to stay silent. Her silence is not passivity but wisdom. She manages with her kindness. She doesn't constantly seek the limelight. She doesn't shout; her tone of voice is moderate. Both her clothing and body language are simple and calm. With her nurturing womb energy, she nourishes and nurtures those around her, both materially and spiritually. This balance softens and refines a woman's soul, making her attractive. A woman who beautifies her inner self first finds the energy and time to care for her outer self later.

Therefore, if you want to increase your feminine energy, seek a healthy and balanced feminine energy. Focus on your inner self, not just your outer self. Because what's inside reflects on the outside.

WHAT ARE THE THINGS YOU ARE AFRAID TO LOSE?

Love, child, mother, work, career, luxury, home, health... Which one are you afraid of losing? That's where your life assignment is. In this life, if you don't educate yourself to let go of what you think you have, you will eventually fall apart.

That's why change scares people. Those who don't want to let go of the old, who desire the same order to continue, resist change. And when the inevitable change comes, they fight with the Divine system. In fact, there is a serious ego and desire here. When some things in their life don't continue as they want, when they can't control them, they don't feel safe. Because their known method is more correct (!) Isn't this the root of most problems we experience in life anyway?

However, change doesn't mean evolving into something else. It's leaving behind what doesn't belong to you and finding yourself. It's leaving behind who you are not. This is awakening to yourself. This is also what the Divine system wants from you.

If you can't grasp this subtle detail, you will try to possess what is entrusted to you, forgetting that it is a trust. You cling tightly to what is entrusted to you. But the world is a place of letting go. Those who cannot realize this do not want to leave their bodies in the world either. They can't die, they can't learn to die. That death is not a beautiful death. Even if they die, their eyes are behind, their souls remain in the limbo. They cannot go to the eternal light. That's why the place we call the grave is actually a place of letting go.

If you stand like a rock in front of the change that is due, the system sometimes forcibly changes. Where you resist to remain as it was, a sudden event comes and you become the change itself. Your life changes without you being in control. So, be willing to let go and change so that what will happen anyway happens easily.

HAVE YOU GOT OUT OF WOUNDED CHILD SYNDROME?

Do you feel resentment and anger towards your parents that you have been neglected? You've probably built or will build a life for yourself far away from them. The reason is spouse, job, living conditions, etc. But what really matters is the energy within a person. That energy carries you away. This is how neglected children neglect their parents. They are so busy that they don't even have the opportunity to search(!)

Deep down, they say to themselves, "I will be different from my mother and father." But a moment comes, and they realize that, no matter how much they distance themselves, they have started to become just like them. They yell at their children like they do, they get angry like they do. They may even find a spouse like the father they're angry with or resemble their mother they get angry with. Or they may find a spouse like the mother they get angry with and resemble their father they're angry with.

As people grow up, they start to look at their parents not with the eyes of a neglected child but with the eyes of an adult. Especially those with children compare the parenting they did themselves with the parenting they saw at home in the past. In fact, they have moved themselves to a higher level, they have become better. But still, there is a strange feeling of similarity inside them. They feel both anger towards themselves for resembling their parents and pride in themselves for escaping from their childhood home and building a better life.

ARE YOU ATTRACTING WHAT YOU LABEL IN YOUR MIND?

Do girls live out their mother's fate? Do boys follow their uncles? Does the pear fall close to the tree? Does the bride fit into her mother-in-law's mold?

There are such sayings that have been ingrained in our subconscious culturally. There is some truth to them. However, in some cases, so many comparisons are made or there is such a belief that it will be so, that the event turns into a self-fulfilling prophecy.

And perhaps, the energy that people fear the most slowly attracts itself into their lives. Then they say things like "I knew it, I said it, it was in me." And thus, they prove their own thought to themselves.

Some things are especially encoded from childhood. By constantly hearing phrases like "just like their aunt, just like their grandfather, they are born with a silver spoon," a person establishes an energetic connection between themselves and the person they are compared to. Instead of living the destiny they have chosen for themselves, they start living a life created by external voices, forming a habit and character that does not belong to them. Later on, they realize that they have not realized their potential, that they have not reached many of their dreams. Because they could not be themselves.

Therefore, stop trying to make your children or yourself like someone else. Stop labeling. Cut the negative ties you have created in your mind. Every thought is also a fateful creation. Of course, genetic and epigenetic factors cannot be denied. There are transmissions from ancestors. But other than these, each of us came into this world to realize our own choices and potential. We can redefine ourselves at any moment. You are not the labels that have been attached to you.

If you must liken your children to someone or if you are going to be likened to someone, accept only the positive aspects of energetically good people, reject the negatives. Because before you know it, what you have accepted has become your truth.

WHAT DOES YOUR PROBLEM WITH AUTHORITY TELL YOU?

Who is the boss, the headman, the state, or the authority figure in your life? If you are in conflict with any of these, there is certainly a message for you there.

A fight that starts with one will be reflected in the other authority figures you encounter in your life. You start arguing with those who set rules. Sometimes you find yourself in a physical, sometimes an internal struggle.

When we delve into the root of this issue, we generally encounter the father figure. Those who have problems with their father in their early years generally continue to have problems with authoritarian figures. However, when we delve deeper and into a more nuanced reading, we see that the problem there is also with Allah. Because at the most basic level, the authority figure who sets rules is Allah. Those who are inwardly in conflict with Allah's system are likely to have problems with authority. The internal rebellion of those who struggle with what life presents them or with the justice system is generally directed towards Allah. It is not easy to realize this and accept it. Some may even appear to be the most vehement defenders of religion. However, those who are in an internal acceptance and divine flow do not need proof of their religious life. Sometimes this internal struggle manifests as, "Look, I am doing so much for you, but you do not care about me, you do not love me" deep down. Some may appear to be serious advocates of authority just to show themselves. But those who rise to the highest also have the potential to sink to the lowest. This state of mind conflicts with the father. They become both the most serious enemy of the father and have the potential to beat up anyone who speaks ill of their father outside. In other words, they experience extremes.

When one makes peace with authority, their power center begins to function correctly. This is an internal acceptance and neutrality. They start to accept and embrace the power given by the Creator. If they accept this power, they make the right decisions. They begin to distinguish between what is beneficial and what is not for themselves. They neither defend their power nor suppress it. They are neither addicted to their father and authority, nor are they their enemies. This state is the state of true balance.

Therefore, if you want to reach your true power, see why you are in conflict with authority, make peace with your father, and ultimately with Allah.

DOES KNOWLEDGE HEAL PEOPLE?

At first, a person does not know what they do not know. They talk a lot, do not let anyone else speak, and their words and comments are endless.

When they realize what they do not know, they start to seek knowledge and still think they know. They continue to tell what they think they know.

They think that knowledge will heal itself.

They give advice to everyone, tell what they know, correct those who do not know. They spread the energy that is not yet settled within themselves.

The veils are thick at the level of comprehension.

Then they stop trying to correct others, stop telling what they know. Because they see that they cannot benefit themselves or others. They become more silent.

This slowing down energy begins to attract topics of truth that they do not know into their lives.

This is where the first step of awakening begins. They realize that what they know is just a drop compared to what they do not know.

Then they understand that they cannot know everything. They accept what they know and what they do not know. They accept themselves as they are.

In this second step of awakening, they begin to let go of the desire to know. They withdraw more into themselves. The veils become thinner.

This is where they start to move from knowledge to wisdom. All knowledge is in the past, while wisdom is in the future.

In the state of wisdom, one understands that new knowledge comes from silence. And in the third step of awakening, they both know everything and know nothing.

True knowledge, truth, and emptiness become apparent. What is needed is found, and it is found in the moment of need.

The veils have been lifted. Every moment is in a state of wonder and witnessing. What a beautiful place that is, not everyone is fortunate enough to experience it.

HOW DO INDIVIDUALS LEANING TOWARDS EXTREMISM BECOME MORE ENTRENCHED IN THEIR BELIEFS?

The Kharijites were a group that did not recognize the caliphate of Hz Ali and considered those who did not share their views as infidels, not granting them the right to life. One day, when they left Basra and came near Nehrewan, they encountered Habbab's son Abdullah, a companion of Muhammed (pbuh) who was traveling with his pregnant wife on a donkey. They invited him to join them, but when they couldn't convince him, they tied him and his wife up and took them as captives. While traveling, they stopped under a date palm tree. At that moment, a date fell to the ground. One of the Kharijites picked it up and ate it. When another Kharijite saw this, he said, "You ate this date unlawfully, without paying for it." Hearing this, the first Kharijite immediately spat out the date. As they continued on their journey, they encountered a pig belonging to a tribe. One of the Kharijites killed the pig, considering it forbidden. When his companions said, "What you did is causing mischief on earth," the Kharijite who killed the pig sought out the owner of the pig and asked for forgiveness. Witnessing these events, Habbab's son said to them, "If you are sincere in your actions, none of your evils should touch me. I am a Muslim and have not done anything evil towards Islam." However, the Kharijites, disregarding his words, brutally killed him and his pregnant wife because they did not join their ranks.

Why did I tell this true story? Sometimes I see very compassionate people towards a cat, a flower, or even a person. Then

I witness the same person treating someone with different views in a hostile manner. I am amazed. Then this story comes to mind. When a person becomes politicized and radicalized in a belief they have embraced, no matter how sensitive they may be in their personal life, they begin to be ruthless towards those who do not think like them. They do not grant the other person the right to live just because they do not think like them. Instead of loving people for being human, the thought of "I will only love them if they think like me" unfortunately dehumanizes people. This is a very interesting psychology, and it does not matter if someone is religious, secular, part of a community, or a political Islamist, nationalist, etc. When they tend towards extremism, they forget divine laws and become hardened. What does our Almighty Allah say in Surah Nisa: "Whoever, whether male or female, does good deeds and is a believer, will enter Paradise, and they will not be wronged even a speck."

In a sacred hadith, Allah (swt) says, "My mercy prevails over My wrath." In other words, according to our belief, love, mercy, and forgiveness are always ahead, but unfortunately, a tremendous rigidity has emerged in our lands. What Allah loves and forgives, humans do not. He does not say, "Who am I?" but becomes capable of tearing apart someone with different views, thinking that they are living very sensitively. The end of this story is known according to divine laws, but still, only Allah knows. Let us be among those who repent.

However, at the root of our Anatolian culture, there is a belief based on love instead of rigidity. What does the Mevlana, who has influenced the heart of the country at one time, say:

Come, come, whoever you are, come again,

Whether you are an infidel, a fire worshiper,

Or an idolater, come again,

Our convent is not a convent of despair,

Even if you have broken your vow a hundred times, come again...

We do not sow any seed on this land other than love...

IN WHICH EMOTION ARE YOU EXCESSIVELY INDULGING?

In our bodies, we also carry the opposite of every emotion. Clinging too much to one emotion is misuse of it. Then, one starts to go to extremes in its opposite. To love and to hate, to like and to judge, to be silent and to talk too much, to show mercy and to get angry, to trust and to panic, to be comfortable and to worry, to be courageous and to be fearful, to be confident and to be passive, to accept and to reject.... In which of these are you going to extremes?

The emotion that one goes to extremes in shows up in their weakest moment. Because you cannot manage the one who goes to extremes. For example, a negative situation we experience with someone often occurs as a reflection of an emotion in us that has gone to extremes. Either you have valued too much, or you have sacrificed too much or made too many concessions, or you have been too afraid and lied, or you have remained too passive, or the relationship balance with the other party has been disrupted because the other party is like that. Whatever goes to extremes becomes the opposite, the balance is disrupted.

When such a situation occurs, it is very easy to blame the other party, to play the role of victim. Saying this does not mean the other party is innocent. What I mean is; if you can say to yourself, "Where did we go to extremes that the relationship balance was disrupted?" then you are taking a real step to heal.

To heal, you need to confront your darkest aspects. Not everyone has the courage to do this. Knowing yourself comes from accepting even your most unpleasant and irritating aspects. If we see ourselves, balance our emotions, and change our perspective, we may find that the energy of the other party also changes.

After learning the lesson here, of course, you can put physical and emotional distances between yourself and people who harm you. This is your most natural right and what you need to do. But the important thing is, have you done your duty and learned your lesson? Or do people change in the scenario of life but the story remains the same?

HEY DERVISH, HOW DID YOU FIND PEACE?

One of the issues that makes people feel trapped the most is the fear of sustenance. Since the world is a material place, people choose to believe in what they see. Because it is easier to believe what you see. People want to see ahead, they want to know how much they will earn next month, they want to calculate when they can buy a house or a car, they want to feel if it will be enough or not. This puts them in a limited mold. Yet sustenance is ready, it is the person who narrows it down.

That's why government jobs and civil service are seem attractive to people. They have a fixed income. Some people in America are like this, too. Those who have a certain annual salary make an annual plan. Their annual holidays and expenses are predetermined. Maybe they are getting enough for themselves, but their awareness of sustenance is also limited. This pushes their lives into routine, that is, into rigidity. They hold on tightly to what they think they have achieved because they think it is hard to obtain. It's hoarding. At the slightest crisis, they fill their garages with food and water. With the addition of psychological traumas, according to research, there are more than 9 million hoarders in America at a pathological level. However, both the giver and the receiver are both Allah. Whoever cannot free their sustenance cannot surrender to the flow. Therefore, they first experience scarcity in their minds. What exists is not enough, it cannot be blessed. They restrict themselves and their families. They cannot share, and even if they do, they cannot live a quality life for themselves.

If a person becomes addicted to what they see with his own eyes, they cannot see that themselves are a miracle. If they constantly make plans and calculations, they cannot open themselves to the miracles of life. They cannot go beyond what they believe and see. Their prayer is like civil service. Since they do not push the limits, they only get up and down, and sense of duty prevents them from feeling their spirit. They cannot rise to the mirage in their prostration.

Taptuk Emre had a line in the TV series Yunus: "Very little of what I believe is visible to the eye." So what do you believe in?

There was a line in the Yunus series by Taptuk Emre: "Very few of what I believe can be seen with the eye." So what do you believe in? Live so beautifully that you also experience the world's blessings beautifully. But don't become dependent as if you will hand over all the trusts tomorrow. First, let go of the anxieties of your mind so that the material flow is both easy and abundant.

They asked the dervish: How did you find peace? The dervish replied: I realized that no one can eat my sustenance, and I calmed down.

WHO ARE THE SAVIORS?

Let's talk about saviors. Those who can't help but help. Those who find themselves wherever there is a wounded person, or those who are drawn to wounded souls. Those who judge what appears to be cruel, those who speak out against the powerful who oppress the weak... What do you try to save the most? The environment, the country, human rights, women, children, or animal rights? Who do you see as the most oppressed in your eyes? Whom do you try to save? And who do you see as very cruel and ruthless?

What about your role? What would happen without you? What if you don't take care of your parents, a patient, paperwork, home, or someone in need? Do you say, "I have to"? Do you think only you can save the situation?

If you have such sharp distinctions and thoughts, you might be in a savior role. And because you are in the energy of the savior, you always find a victim/sufferer to save and help in your life. The victim always finds their savior.

So who wants to be saved? The insecure. Those whose trust has been shaken somewhere begin to see the world as unsafe. Actually, the trust in the Divine system is shaken at its core. They see the world as unjust. Then they try to become saviors. In other words, they play God.

Is it always like this? No. The intention is not to replace God, of course. But there may be a conflict with the Divine system deep down.

Atheists can be the toughest advocates for human or environmental rights.

However, there is balance in the Divine system. Good is balanced with evil, evil with good. Behind what seems unjust to us, there is tremendous mercy. Like the story of Merkez Efendi... If we look at the universe with that perspective, we won't find anything to change. Everything is in its place, as it should be. If humans disrupt their balance somewhere, the balance of the system is sometimes in the hands of the oppressor. An event that seems unjust to us may have brought us into balance in an area we cannot see about ourselves. The laws of Divine justice do not work as humans know them. When humans cannot see this, they seek worldly justice.

So should we not help?

We will certainly help. As much as we can. But look at the intention behind it. Do you think no one else will help if you don't? Do you know the person you're helping is a tyrant? Do you think you can save the victim with the help you provide? Do you judge others while helping? Or do you only do your best, knowing that the one you help also has an owner, that their suffering is known to their Creator, that every victim has their own test and destiny, and by witnessing and knowing this, do you only do what you can?

You are only a means. Lives and hearts are in the hands of Allah. If He wills, we live; if He wills, we find guidance; if He wills, we become a means. He is the Savior, the Forgiver, and the One who gives the test. We are only servants. We have as much life and sensitivity as a butterfly in this world.

WHO TAKES ON THE ROLE OF THE VICTIM?

We had talked about those in life who play the role of the savior. Now let's talk about those in the role of the victim.

Is the helm of your life in your hands? Or do you think you're being directed by someone else? In other words, are you passive? Do you constantly think about the past and its issues? Do you believe you're getting sick because of others? Are you looking for a savior? Then you might be in the victim mindset.

Those who see themselves as victims usually blame others for all the negatives in their lives. They do their best, they try, but no one around them understands them. It's not themselves that need to change, it's the outside world. Family, mother, father, spouse, siblings, friends, boss, government, etc., are to blame. In these accusations, they cannot see themselves or the message of the events. It's a state of low consciousness.

For example, someone who has been wronged in the past sometimes constantly recounts that pain and throws a hook into the past. Then, because they are constantly nourished by that place, they become addicted to it. Those who live with past pains prefer the victim role. Some even attract attention this way. They are not even aware themselves, but they feed off the victimhood or trouble they have fallen into. They define themselves through this pain. Even though events and stories change, their position and way of expressing themselves do not change. Even though they constantly complain about their situation, they are quite willing to remain in the victim role.

This 'victimhood' puts the person into a cycle. And their energy enters into the creation of other stories where they will be victims. The person becomes blind to both the outside and themselves. So, the person's biggest harm is to themselves again.

And then there is the anger of not being able to prove oneself right, which fuels the fire of revenge within. They cannot forgive. And some even poison their own children with this fire, leaving them a legacy of negative energy. The child becomes an enemy of the one who did not cause anything to themselves, whether it be a child, a spouse, a friend, or a relative, who did not cause anything to themselves. The child, unable to fulfill themselves with this burden, lags behind in their life tasks and struggles to get their life in order.

So why do people get into this psychology? Because the victim psychology is easier than facing oneself and the troubles one experiences. It is more comforting to see and blame someone else's fault than to see one's own fault. Also, because they do not know how to heal themselves and cannot fight in this state, blaming others is a kind of survival effort. Because some people cannot live with their own dark side.

The cure, however, lies in being able to see oneself in every aspect and to face one's wounds. When experiencing trouble, before blaming the outside, asking, "Why did I attract this event to myself? What is my message?" is the beginning of healing. Someone may have really hurt you and you may have become a victim. But either because you didn't know your own worth and were made to feel worthless, or because you made this feeling fuel, or because you were trying to attract attention, or because you fell behind in your life tasks and life assigned someone to speed you up. Of course, stories are different, and observations are different... But don't stay there, don't keep telling the same story like a broken record, deliver your lesson and move on. Life wants this from you. It doesn't mean those who harm you are right.

But there's an important point you need to understand: What we experience is about us...

WHO IS OVERLY EMPATHETIC?

Some people internalize the suffering of others so deeply that they feel as if they are experiencing the same thing themselves. Some people even feel the same pain in their bodies. They cannot detach from the event they have watched or heard about; they find themselves in the middle of the event. You might say, "What's wrong with that, they're providing support." On the contrary, this state strengthens healthy active listening and support.

Sometimes, all a person suffering wants is for someone to be there, not someone giving advice or someone who shares the same pain. Constantly giving advice is unhealthy communication. If there is no request or question in the problem area, just being a listener is healthy communication.

Those who constantly complain about the suffering of others are strangers to themselves. If they also pity the other side's experiences, they may be swimming in dangerous waters. Because pity belongs to Allah alone. No one is more merciful than Allah. Every person is on a unique journey of self-realization according to their potential. The person is experiencing the pain they need to experience according to their potential. Because the compassionate person may forget this, they can be tested by saying "come, experience it" regarding the subject they pity. Because they internalize it so much, they may attract something similar into their own lives. Because underneath the feeling of pity, there may be judgment and a hidden ego. This also complicates the task of life.

This doesn't mean "ignore those in distress." If you can help, of course, you should, and we should. But constantly pitying someone, lamenting, and helping indicate a lack of understanding of the Divine system.

When a person is primarily responsible for themselves and has their own soul world to cultivate, struggling in others' pain or constantly looking at someone else's happiness is a waste of time. Fulfill yourself. Where are you in your servitude, in your spiritual development? Look inside yourself first. Otherwise, you won't see the blessings given to you, and you will be subjected to another test to see them.

In my opinion, this is how the mathematics of life works. Actually, this equation is not difficult, but when people get stuck on the manure in the rose garden, they keep suffering in the rose garden...

What can we say; may our requests come easily, with love, happiness, and understanding. May we find peace in our meetings.

WHY DOES THE HEART FEEL, YET THE HUMAN DOESN'T UNDERSTAND?

In a study conducted by the Heart Math Institute, it was researched how people's hearts emit frequencies when looking at good and bad photographs. The results were interesting. When seeing a beautiful photograph, the heart's frequency would increase, while it would decrease when seeing a bad photograph, even before the bad photograph was shown. So, the heart could feel a photograph that would make it sad or affect it without seeing it. It's that frequency that makes us human.

Before a societal event occurs, many people sometimes feel collectively stressed, suffocated, or a heaviness in their souls. They may even have stressful dreams. We call this collective consciousness. It's the unique frequency that our hearts feel together. If something difficult is coming, we feel it. Because Allah created our program this way. For example, before earthquakes, many people feel stressed in different ways.

Nature events, for this reason, give great lessons to humanity. Feeling it before the event softens hearts, brings them closer to Allah. When that moment comes, whether you experience the event or not, people directly transition to the yin energy. They become silent, motionless, and surrender. That's what the Creator wants anyway. The person surrenders to this energy that comes over them first. Then they do what they can. It's not the time to blame or find the culprit. The real duty of a person is this: "First, receive the message," says the Divine system. Then you demand your right, pointing out those who didn't give their right in the circle of causes, those who violate social rights.

So, what could our messages be? This realm is a temporary inn. You enter from one door, you exit from the other. We all have a time. We are not eternal in this worldly life where we embody. But how quickly we forget. We stick as if we will never die, as if we will never lose, as if we own everything. We break hearts, belittle, exclude, alienate, behave recklessly and rudely, withhold our love or a kind word, pollute and selfishly consume nature.

Think about yourself in this context. What have you neglected, given up, been selfish about, remained silent, closed your eyes to, compromised, ignored, in which matters did you violate rights or not stand up for your own rights, supported those without merit, and what will you do next? Don't immediately assume the victim role by saying, "Oh, they violated my rights!" After all, we are in a collective energy field. Messages come not only for those experiencing the event but also for all of us who witness the event, individually for each of us. Our task is to receive this message and move on to the next stage. Otherwise, the tasks will repeat, and so will the troubles.

WHY DO SOME PEOPLE LIKE NEGATIVITY?

Some people are not motivated by peace and happiness. Their fuel is negativity, and they feed off of it. For example, some people stay in a state of illness because that's where they get attention. They can't say "I need attention," but they frequently get sick. Some people get angry over the smallest things. They can't say "I can't express myself," so they try to get things done by yelling. Some people act like they know everything about everything. They can't say "I wasn't approved of as a child, please approve of me now," so they try to be dominating and in the spotlight everywhere. Some people are constantly being cheated or having their belongings stolen. They can't say "I can't control my own space, I lie to myself," so they make others around them fulfill this role. Some suffer from unrequited love, some get depressed over small things, some are always oppressed, some are always on the victimized side. Furthermore, these individuals, although they constantly complain about their situations, are quite willing to remain in the role of the victim.

In essence, what they complain about the most is often what they actually need. Because they are not even aware of it, but they express themselves best in this way. They are stuck in that state like a child clinging to a toy. Even if they cry for help, if you take that state away from them, they will eagerly find a similar one again. They might run away from an abusive father, only to find an abusive husband. Because they have not understood or realized why they are in that state.

After staying in this state for a long time, it becomes part of their routine, a part of their character. This is what feeding off negativity is. It is being stuck in the vicious cycle of a pain or a situation that has come to shape them.

To move to a higher level, the realm of peace, one must first realize that state, accept themselves, and then intend to willingly let go of that state. You can also seek help. Then, whenever a similar situation arises, one must first look at why they haven't said goodbye to that state and examine the residues that have not been cleansed from within. Then, without dwelling too much in that emotion, one must strive to pass through it.

Even if that state returns, you will have learned to deal with it immediately. And before you know it, you will no longer be affected by what happens. You might even forget both the pains and those who caused them.

For those who set out with good intentions, there will always be plenty of divine help coming their way.

IS YOUR MIND STILL ON THOSE YOU LOST?

Do you have a story of loss that you often think about or talk about? It could be about a loved one, your career, your emotions, your finances, or your youth. I will focus on what happens after the loss, not why it occurred. Remaining in that loss or pain and constantly expressing it keeps the pain alive. Moreover, it affects both the person and their environment. Especially what is told to children leaves them with emotional inheritance and burden.

Living that pain constantly does not lead the story to a good place, but rather to a worse place. And here, the victim card comes into play. Sometimes, a person unknowingly plays this victim card, either to others or to themselves, to pity themselves. Those who play the victim card to others may also have a desire for attention. By constantly expressing and using the existing pain, they can draw attention to themselves. They exist through that pain. This is very important. Because these individuals, even if the story changes in other events, do not change their way of expressing it. This 'victimhood' puts the person into a cycle. The person becomes blind to both the outside world and themselves. In other words, the person's biggest harm is to themselves again.

In cases where the loss is not externalized but remembered and experienced within oneself, it could be the ego. Because without surrender regarding the loss, there is no acceptance. The issue there is not the loss, it is the person themselves. Instead of the loss, they have surrendered to the emotions they could not satisfy within themselves. They could not manage their life as they wished, they could not control their past loss. Here, too, the person's biggest harm is to themselves again.

So what do we do in such a situation?

We will know that both what comes and what goes are for our own good. Not just in words, but with understanding and sincerity. If you have approved and come to live the life you will experience in the spiritual realm, if you have said "yes" to your destiny in the world life, then "being" is the best. If you remain in what is lost, you cannot find what is new. Pass through the past losses with surrender. "Your Lord will give you, and you will be satisfied" (Ad-Duha 5).

WHAT LEVEL IS YOUR AWARENESS?

People's levels of awareness vary greatly. Some always blame the outside world for all the negativity they experience. They perpetually feel like victims. It's as if they do everything they can and strive, but the people around them never understand them. They believe it's not themselves who need to change, but the people outside—whether it's family, parents, spouse, siblings, friends, boss, or even the government. These people do not accept the problems within themselves. This is a state of low consciousness.

Another level of awareness involves a person who, to some extent, holds themselves responsible for the negativity they experience or witness around them. They begin to say, "We are all to blame" for societal issues. They notice the areas where they haven't taken responsibility. But this is still not a sufficient level of consciousness because they still see most of the fault in others. They haven't fully turned inward and haven't yet recognized their own shortcomings.

The third group, who surpass these two levels of awareness, completely takes responsibility for their lives and what happens to them. They stop looking for someone to blame and first move into a state of acceptance. This is the beginning of an internal awakening. They work on improving themselves, realizing that change and transformation start not with others but with themselves. They start to see everyone as a mirror. This level marks the beginning of inner miracles because awakening begins with seeing oneself. And this awakening is the key to setting one's life on the right path.

People who pass through this third level of awareness stop saying "I" and start saying "we." They no longer expect anything in return for what they do for others. They understand that every event and being is invisibly connected to one another, and they recognize the existence of a higher consciousness, the Creator, who is above all. This is a state of surrender. They begin to see events from a bird's-eye view, witnessing what lies behind them. They exist in pure love, in inner balance. They no longer seek miracles; they themselves become the miracle. This is the level of development that humans must ultimately reach.

Some people experience each of these levels of awareness one by one. Some leap to a higher level after a shocking event in their lives. And some get stuck on one level for years. Although divine assistance reaches every person, the level of their awareness depends on their individual will.

CAN'T THOSE WHO CANNOT DIE IN THE PAST BE BORN INTO THE NEW?

I read an expression "the dead living in the past." It's used for those who are stuck in the past and still living there in their inner world. Even though seasons and years have passed, calling those who still talk about past issues "the dead" isn't entirely wrong. They haven't been reborn into the new, haven't experienced the new...

These people also tire those around them along with themselves. They project the traumas and burdens of the past onto those around them every day, just as they live it. Then they blame others for being insensitive. With a fire circle built around their small world, they want to burn the whole world. Because of this energy, they don't have many friends around them.

Others may not have experienced as much pain as they have, but no one should have to carry another's burden.. Everyone is experiencing their test according to their caliber. Constantly blaming others and making others share in this pain without seeing the lesson life gives is not understanding it. In America, there is a saying, "God uses the flawed for a perfect system." Those who constantly point fingers at the flawed become a part of the flawed, but they don't even realize it.

So, it's up to humans to be able to see the order hidden within the disorder of the world. Those who constantly get stuck in disorder cannot read life.

Yet even seasons are such a beautiful lesson for us. Night ends, morning comes, winter ends, spring begins. The tree that sheds its leaves sprouts again. The seedling grows, the farmer harvests, but it gives vegetables from its roots. In other words, life leaves the old behind and is born anew moment by moment. Our world of thought and emotion is also like this. Those who don't learn the lesson of life live in the past and cannot be reborn into the new. Those who learn the lesson of life don't become the dead of the past, but they die in the past and are reborn into the future.

So where are you in life? Are you living in the past and wasting time, or have you already set off towards the future?

WHERE DO YOU BELONG?

Do you have a place or environment where you say, "This is where I feel I belong"? It could be your childhood home, your village or hometown, a job, a gym, a university—any place where you feel good and complete. The place where you feel you belong is where you fulfill yourself and feel satisfied.

Your soul knows what is right for you. If you have experienced that place, you are naturally drawn to it. If you haven't experienced it, you must first learn to listen to your soul. Those who do not know themselves and do not listen to their soul do not know what they love or what their talents are. Due to this alienation from themselves, they cannot feel like they belong anywhere.

Those who do not know themselves are those who run away from themselves. So why does a person run away from themselves?

Knowing oneself is difficult. Because on the journey of self-discovery, you not only find where you belong, your loved ones, and your talents, but you also confront your darkest sides. Most people do not want to accept their dark sides. If they see their negative sides, they lower the guard they have raised against the outside world. While lowering your guard may be perceived as weakness, that is exactly where you truly are, where you see yourself. That's when the sense of belonging starts to develop. But not everyone has the courage for this challenging journey.

This is why the spiritual journey that a person embarks on to know themselves is called the hero's journey.

POSTPONING YOUR LIFE?

One night in my dream, I was looking up at the sky. There were clouds made of rainbows. Just like in cartoons, there were unicorns and castles above the clouds. People were climbing up to the clouds from the ground using steep stairs. I also started climbing up excitedly. Then I looked down. I saw my children who couldn't climb up the stairs. I had to decide whether to leave them and continue climbing to see that dream world or stay with them and miss this opportunity. And of course, I chose my children and went down to be with them.

When I woke up in the morning, I thought about this dream a lot. My first reaction was this: I need to postpone and wait for my dreams about some spiritual issues because of my children. Then, when I talked about this dream with a friend, I realized that my interpretation was not entirely correct. In fact, I saw my children as obstacles to realizing my dreams. My higher consciousness had misled me in my interpretation.

In reality, my children were not obstacles to anything. On the contrary, they were the means for my dreams to come true. The obstacle in front of my dreams was my thoughts. My dream was not showing me what I needed to do but rather my state of mind.

I know that many mothers and some fathers feel like I do. There are many mothers who cannot see themselves, realize their dreams, or ask "where am I in my life?" because they have devoted themselves to their children and their home. To them, I can say the following sentences that I say to myself: You are exactly where you need to be. That little soul is entrusted to you. One of your life tasks is to guide them and allow them to teach your soul. You made such an agreement in the spiritual realm and chose each other. Karmically, this was what you needed to do. You needed this life for your spiritual evolution. Yes, this is exactly what your soul needed. It could not have been any other way. Every choice you made was ultimately necessary.

You don't need to feel guilty or delayed. Your dreams would only be satisfied in this way. Experiencing motherhood, raising your children, and growing your soul with them required you to evolve rapidly. Because motherhood changes a woman completely. Similarly, fatherhood changes fathers a lot. It melts their rigidity, dulls their ego, and balances their egos. It teaches them compassion, sacrifice, sleeplessness, exhaustion for others, unconditional love, and attention. A woman later uses these feelings for the world. Otherwise, experiencing and learning these feelings could only have been possible in years of serious seclusion and life in a seminary.

If you feel like a hindered parent, go to your children. Hug them and be grateful for these gifts given to you. The rest is trivial talk...

WAS THE PAST BETTER THAN TODAY?

I come across sentences longing for the past. They say the past was better, more sincere. "Whose past? What kind of past?" I ask myself... Everyone's past wasn't the same.. Some things were not as sincere or natural as they are depicted to be.

There is a scene in the movie Forrest Gump. Jenny, who visits her childhood home years later, tries to tear down her old house with rocks she picked up from the ground. Then she falls to the ground and starts crying. What had she experienced, felt that years later she was trying to vent her anger by tearing down her house.. That's why not everyone longs for the past. In fact, there are those who do their best to forget.

To be honest, there are good memories, but the world didn't have such a glorious past. A group of people suffered, were subjected to genocide, displaced from their homes in the world. Innocents died in power wars, people suffered from poverty and hunger. I'm not even talking about women's and children's rights. And I'm not even mentioning women who resigned themselves to fate, children who were subjected to violence and abuse, neighbors who knew but remained silent and complicit in violence...

My intention is not to blame the past. All the societal and individual pains experienced for the evolution of humanity. They are still happening. But it's easy for others to say from a distance. Those who live know. Their lessons and outcomes contributed to the whole. Every pain experienced in the past became a lesson for the world and developed collective consciousness. And some things will continue until the world's time is up. Because humanity, if it doesn't choose to elevate its consciousness, if it lingers in the world's enjoyable and comfortable zone, cannot complete the world's assignments and evolve. Then the world accelerates evolution with pains and traumas.

It's not my intention to darken the mood. But let's admit it, there is no past that will be glorified or mythologized. Human beings only live their own time. It is up to humans to make the present moment beautiful and to love it. So, one must appreciate the value of this time. To leave beautiful memories for oneself and for their children, one must strive today. Live in the beauty of today, not in the corridors of the past. In short, love your time and what it offers you…

ARE THERE ANY THINGS YOU INSIST?

Most people complain about their life circumstances and luck. Yes, these are influential, but actually, the most important thing that determines our lives is our choices. Whatever we have experienced, we have lived the sum and consequence of our past choices. This is what is called fate.

Sometimes you made an agreement with a word, sometimes you chose laziness when you had the freedom to act. Sometimes with negligence, sometimes with a right you entered, sometimes by giving too much value to others, sometimes by spending the energy you should have spent on yourself on others, right there, we determined our lives. We allowed the troubles that happened to us. We needed those troubles for our minds to come to us.

But sometimes what we wanted with good intentions did not happen. That's when we were protected. In such times, know that divine will has protected us from ourselves. It was a request that you didn't yet need or that would harm you when you got it. Maybe you didn't like what was given to you, but rest assured, you were reciprocated with something better than what you wanted. One of the tasks there is; When you are happy with what you want, do you accept what you don't want when you experience it? Could you realize that there was something better than what was offered to you? Or did you rebel and fight against what you had?

Perhaps because life was horizontal, it needed to evolve, perhaps a little silence, perhaps a little accountability, perhaps a little withdrawal, or need to be alone. Pain and sorrow are sometimes a remedy. Whenever you went overboard in a matter, you would call its opposite into your life. Then the situation that seemed wrong to you came to heal you and meet a need.

Sometimes we do not know how what we insist on will harm us. Perhaps what we need is just the opposite. As Rumi said, "How do you know that the ground under you is not better than the sky?" So, today, even now, what are you determining your future with your choices and words? What are you insisting on? What are you choosing, what are you accepting? Look at what you demand from this perspective.

DID YOU BUILD YOUR OWN PARADISE?

The story goes that before the flood, Prophet Noah warns his people and informs them about the ark he has built. An elderly woman who believed in him occasionally brings him some milk and reminds him, "O Noah, I believe in your God, do not forget to take me aboard the ship if the flood comes." When the time comes, Prophet Noah takes those who believe in him and a pair of every animal onto the ark. However, his wife and son do not believe him and refuse to board the ship. And the flood comes. The water rises forty cubits above the highest mountains. None of those who did not board the ship survive. After the flood recedes, according to the tale, the ark lands on Mount Judi.

Prophet Noah realizes that he has forgotten the elderly woman, but it is too late. However, one day, the elderly woman comes to him safe and sound. When she reminds him again, "O Noah, do not forget to take me aboard the ship if there is a flood," Noah asks in astonishment, "The flood has already happened, we have landed on land. Where have you been hiding?" The woman replies, "I did not see anything, I did not leave my own home."

Noah, surprised, asks, "Did you not see any water at all?" The woman answers, "One day when I went to milk my cow, its hoof was a little muddy. I did not see anything else."

Whether this story is true or not, we cannot say. Let's focus on what it makes us think about. In the world, with the economy, wars, health, education, and social life, fears and delusions are increasing day by day. But some people can live in their own paradise amidst this chaos. The flood outside becomes mud under your feet. As long as one's inner world is suitable for that paradise. As long as our trust and reliance on Allah are complete.

WALKING WHICH PATHS SEEM DAUNTING TO YOU?

Are you not satisfied with the job you do, the field you study, the school you attend, or the life you create? Then you may not have met the path you needed to follow in your life journey. Let me explain a little more what I mean.

We have two fateful paths. First; the way the soul knows. Perhaps our ancestors, and therefore our souls connected to them, experienced this path in past lives. Latter; the new way we must see and experience. The soul is drawn to what it knows, that is, to the past, but it may not be successful there. Because your consciousness has experienced it before and that's why your life task may not be there.

If you are wondering how to find the path you need to follow, look at the new paths you encounter throughout your life that intimidate you. What were you afraid of, what forced you, what did you avoid, what did you not want to face? Have those ways and subjects grown in your eyes? Did it seem unattainable at times? Maybe your duty was to go there. That's why most people become lazy, waste their potential in old ways and become unhappy. If you actually find where you are going, even falling on that path will make you happy and your tiredness will give you joy.

That's why everyone's life purpose and satisfaction are different. Because our life tasks are different. Set out to find your true purpose..

SOUR OR SWEET?

From the film Vanilla Sky, there's a wonderful line that sticks in my mind: "Without the sour, the sweet isn't as sweet."

Sometimes, we invite sour feelings into our lives that are the opposite of our sweet feelings. Because we're unaware of our own needs and what we invite in, we blame external factors. We think we only experience difficult emotions because of others.

However, if we didn't have those sour feelings, we wouldn't fully appreciate the value of our sweet feelings. For a person to develop understanding in the simulation of the world, they need opposites. After all, everything is known by its opposite.

So instead of blaming external factors for an event, when we start asking ourselves the right questions, the course of our lives changes.

If we ask ourselves questions like, "Why did I need this event? What point about myself is this event showing me? What weakness is it here to strengthen?" then the right answers and sweet feelings quickly come into our lives.

Because whatever we experience, we're experiencing it for the development of our understanding. And when we look at life with a positive outlook, we invite beauty in.

DO I HAVE THE PROBLEM?

I had a friend whom I hadn't had a chance to meet for a long time. She called me; she's starting a new job and wanted to call before things get too busy, to thank me for the posts I've written on Instagram. She mentioned that since she started incorporating the phrase "with ease" into her life, she has been talking about how some things that seemed difficult actually became easier.

"I used to get annoyed by what you wrote at first," she said. "Statements like 'look within, the outside is a reflection of ourselves, if we change, our environment changes' used to irritate me." "Over time, I understood what you meant. When I turned inward and changed myself in some matters, I saw that my environment changed too," she said. And we talked extensively about these topics. She had researched and read more about the topics I briefly touched upon, and the conversation flowed easily when we were on the same wavelength.

Talking to her reminded me of my old self. There comes a period in our lives when there's a flow that bothers us, and we begin to search. Initially, what we encounter in response to our questions can be annoying. We don't want to accept it. Because the answers to our questions are beyond our judgments and patterns, beyond what we know. We say, "Isn't the outside at fault at all? Is every problem with me?" and yes, we get annoyed. But as the window of truth opens slowly, we start to say, "What exists in the universe exists in me/to Adam," referring to ourselves. We realize that everything we experience, watch, and hear is a reflection of ourselves and what we judge. The war you're watching might be about what you're fighting within yourself. Those who make you feel worthless might be related to your lack of self-worth. Those trying to crush you might be related to the pressure you put on yourself. It might be a little, it might be a lot, but that feeling might be about you. Instead of getting angry at others and getting into fights, take a look inside, see what's there.

From that moment on, we begin to accept even those who hurt us as teachers. We know how to keep our distance from those who give off negative energy. We become courageous and know our own value.

After embarking on this path of awakening and evolution, there is no turning back. It's always a path moving forward. Sometimes, there's a lesson we need to learn, so we stop for a while. Until we understand. Then we continue with an upward momentum. For those who embark on this path and ask themselves the right questions, the answers come quickly.

So, let's awaken those *latife sleeping within us, let's awaken them and embark on the path, what do you think?

*Latife: A term of Sufism that points to the divine essence in humans.

BUT THE PROBLEM IS NOT WITH ME, IT'S WITH THE OTHER PERSON!

Are you one of those who say, "I'm trying to improve and heal myself, but the problem is not with me. It's my spouse/mother/child who needs to change, but they don't listen to me. They have no effort or awareness"?

If so, let me tell you the first rule: You can only fix yourself, not others. If a person has a desire to improve and heal, they will do so. We can pray for someone, guide and help those who seek it, and be a means if the time is right. Hearts are in the hands of Allah.

But if we start to interfere in someone's life to fix them, we make things more difficult. In fact, we may become part of their confusion and trial. For example, many parents are tested with their children. When we act like their owners and hinder their development, we usually end up spoiling our relationship with them. If we don't allow them to fall and make mistakes in some challenging situations, the life lesson they haven't learned will be postponed and may be repeated later, perhaps in a more difficult way. And the pain will be even greater for the parent along with the child. What you want to fix may be that person's need for growth.

Therefore, a person should always first look into their own life mirror. Those who constantly try to check the mirrors of those around them may end up having to struggle with both their own life and many broken and scattered mirrors.

Letting go lifts a great burden off our shoulders. Let go of the rush to fix and save those around you. Look at whether you have been saved. Trust in Allah, the owner of everyone. We are not more merciful than Allah.

WHAT DID YOUR BIRTH TELL YOU?

When your birthday comes, what is your mood like? Do you feel low, or do you become very cheerful? Do you want someone to celebrate your birthday, prepare surprises? Or do you prefer to be alone and quiet?

Do you like the season you were born in, or does it make you feel cramped? Did you born on a rainy or snowy day? How do you feel about that season now? For instance, I was born in November. It's my favorite month. I love the transition from autumn to winter, the chill in the air. Summer doesn't make me happy. The weather was cool on the day I was born too. When they gave me to my mother, my father took me in his arms and kissed my forehead. It seems I was accepted at my birth. That's why I made peace with the month I was born. I'd like my birthday to be remembered and celebrated, deep down, and my heart fills with joy as my birthday approaches.

Our mood on our birthdays is therefore closely related to our birthday. It is related to our birth and our mother's mood at the time of our birth. Did you feel valued or worthless at birth? How did your surroundings react when you were born? What was the first word you heard? What have you encoded since that day? That's why listen to your birth story from your mother repeatedly. You'll solve many things in your life that you couldn't understand about yourself.

Isn't life like this anyway? Know and solve yourself. Our world fate and duties started at birth. If you make readings about your life from that day to today, you will accept yourself more. You will understand more why you came to this world, where you came from, and where you are going. You understand yourself, you see your true self... This is what evolves and grows us.

WHY DON'T I HAVE FRIENDS AROUND ME LIKE I USED TO?

Why don't I have friends around me like I used to? Do I feel very lonely now? Do you find yourself asking these questions often? Then you've probably started pulling one foot away from the world and towards the spiritual realm.

Our Prophet says that if one day is the same as the other, you will be in loss. So, it would be futile to compare yourself to the past and question why things aren't the same. You are constantly experiencing new things, gaining new experiences, and advancing spiritually. In the past, you needed to experience social environments to develop your soul and emotions with other people. Now, you need to withdraw into your inner world and make friends with yourself. Perhaps it's time to love yourself and return to your neglected true self.

Especially for those approaching or over the age of 40, this is an inevitable end. You no longer have many friends with whom you can confidently discuss everything. You have a few close friends with whom you have beautiful conversations. And you become selective even with them. You may prefer to spend more time alone at home. You want to withdraw from the crowd and look up at the sky. This is quite normal and should be the case for many of you, the time has come to search for yourself.

After the age of 40, like our Prophet, it's time to withdraw into your inner self to receive your spiritual revelations from God. Because you have completed half of your worldly experience. Now is the time to prepare for the eternal world. That's why worldly pleasures and social environments no longer bring the same joy. Those who chase after these pleasures after 40 have either experienced the fear and panic of facing this reality or have not had enough worldly experience in the past. Therefore, they become obsessed with money, lust, status, career, ostentation, aesthetics, and material possessions, becoming selfish. But this state does not suit them. "Your best young people are those who resemble your old people. And your worst old people are those who resemble your young people." This hadith somewhat explains this. Experience the world but don't become its slave. Learn to let go of what is due, accept old age, be serious. Forty teaches us this.

The Qur'an also praises the age of 40: "And when he attained his full strength and was [mentally] mature, We bestowed upon him judgement and knowledge. And thus do We reward the doers of good." (Surah Al-Ahqaf 46:15)

In short, if you are feeling lonely from now on, instead of saying, "Why don't I have many friends anymore?" asking questions like "How can I be friends with myself? How can I engage in righteous deeds for the rest of my life?" can have a more healing effect.

IS YOUR ENERGY FLOWING IN THE RIGHT DIRECTION?

When a person sets new goals for themselves, they immediately think about where to direct their energy and prepare a list. However, if they were to do the opposite, they might be more successful. Instead of thinking about where to spend their energy, if they find out for what or for whom they spent the most energy in the past, they can chart their path better and more efficiently. Think about it, who or what did you invest the most energy in? Sit down and write them down one by one. Think about who and what you have allocated your energy to so far.

A person's energy is not infinite in the world; it is a limited source of energy. Because every person does not know how to connect themselves to the infinite Divine source, let that limitless flow to themselves. Especially in the material realm of the world, the physical is important. The body gets tired and cannot bear too much burden. Therefore, people who do not behave smartly about where to spend their limited energy also become exhausted.

Think again about the energy and effort you have spent throughout the year from this perspective. Did they return to you positively? Did they increase your life energy and quality? Or did they consume and pull you down? How much progress have you made on the road you have come? Have you improved, or have you deteriorated? What does the future hold for you? How do you feel? Do what you've given back in your relationships make you happy?

If you have always been the giving side in your relationships and feel that your energy and effort are depleted, it's time to move the stones, that is, to remove those people and things from your list.

Take the energy you spent there and use it for yourself first in the coming year, and give the rest to the deserving relationships and tasks. Perhaps it's time to close some doors to open new ones. This way, you will have used your finite energy infinitely in the right place.

Be in the energy fields where you grow, not where you consume and decrease. If you want your energy to be more than enough for yourself, your spouse, your children, your loved ones, and the things you love, listen to what I'm saying. Otherwise, every new year passes by with hopes and plans that have run out of energy, unfulfilled. And you age aggressively, and life ends unhappily...

SOMEWHERE THERE IS A GIRL WITH A PEACH

I watched a documentary called "World War II: From the Frontlines". They cleaned up and colorized many previously unreleased, low-quality images. It was an objective documentary. Through the witnesses and footage, I once again understood the ordeal the world went through.

There was a scene that caught my attention. Hitler, allied with Mussolini, declares war on the British forces in South Africa. Interestingly, while Europe was being crushed under the Nazi pressure, Libya and Egypt fiercely resisted the German soldiers. They were tired of the colonial rule of England. The Germans brought the British soldiers they captured in Africa to a port in Southern Italy. The exhausted soldiers, emaciated from hunger and fatigue, were paraded in front of the people. The Italian people punched and spat on the soldiers.

One memory of a British prisoner of war named Ray deeply affected me. He recounted, "Our condition was very bad. We were both hungry and extremely tired. Many of my friends had died on the roads. The people hit us and spat on us. Then, a young girl came out of the crowd and placed a large peach in my hand. Then, she turned back to the crowd and disappeared. I covered my mouth with my hands and ate it. I had never tasted anything more delicious in my life. Then, I started crying. When you feel like the whole world is against you, and everything is going wrong, I think of a girl somewhere with a peach. It was a wonderful feeling. It gave me hope that things could change."

During this period, when we look at the memories of those who survived the genocide camps, we see a common feature:

they had hope for survival and a belief that everything would change. They found something to hold on to, something that gave them hope, in the hardest moments. According to a scientific study, some of those predicted to live for 4 to 6 months have lived longer. When we look at their common traits, they all have someone at home who keeps their hope and zest for life alive. Some have a spouse, some have children or grandchildren, some have a dog waiting at home. They cling tightly to life for them, extending their lives.

There are hopeful, innocent, good people everywhere, pushed to various places by circumstances. And God protects them without distinction. It is humans who make distinctions. In the toughest moments, even when you feel like you've reached the end, there is always a light at the end of the darkness. The darkest point of darkness is where the light begins. So whenever you feel trapped, even when you think you can't find a way out, keep hope alive. Maybe when you least expect it, a girl with a peach will be sent to you from within that light.

DO YOU KNOW THE QUEEN OF THE NIGHT?

Do you know the flower that blooms only once a year? Not for a couple of months, not for a week, not even for a day. I'm talking about a flower that blooms only once a year, as the sun sets and fades at dawn. It's so rare, so beautiful. This flower, known as the "queen of the night" in America, the "beauty under the moon" in Japan, and the "flower of victory" in Indonesia, is actually a cactus flower. It only displays its beauty for one night and then closes and withers until the next year. So, it uses all its splendor in just one night. When it blooms, it emits a soothing, beautiful scent around it. A scent that few people have the opportunity to smell. According to Indian belief, prayers made during the hours when this flower is open are accepted. Very few people know when this flower blooms and fades. Finding this flower in a regular flower shop is impossible. It's a rare species and is very expensive. Naturally, it makes you feel special, the queen of the night.

I thought of this flower while thinking about a topic. Sometimes, you shouldn't present your knowledge, talents, and beautiful and unique aspects to everyone who comes your way. Even if your intention is good, you can harm those you try to help. Many people are not ready to encounter such well-intentioned actions or that knowledge. Or they simply don't appreciate them. I'm not talking about a person's value or uniqueness; I'm talking about the waste of knowledge and time that is unnecessarily exposed. Those who seek should find it. When you present it to someone who doesn't seek it, what you present becomes trampled underfoot. Because they don't appreciate its value. That's why the principle of appropriateness is very important. You should know how to speak and how to remain silent at the right time. Don't tell what you know to someone who doesn't ask immediately. Your well-intentioned act or that knowledge can turn into wasted energy for you. What you say as "Let them know, learn, understand, benefit" is often not understood. You are not doing them a favor. By presenting it to someone who doesn't seek it, it loses its value in you. Inappropriateness consumes the energy you should first spend on yourself.

When you truly find balance, sort out your inner world, and turn it into a flower garden, your fragrance will spread around you. People will start to circle around you and ask for what you have to offer. That's why sometimes you should be like the queen of the night. When the time comes, present all your treasures to those who seek, to those who search and find.

We are all precious, my friends. Human beings are the noblest of creatures. But a person determines their own value. When you pay attention to where you are, who you are with, what you talk about, what you listen to, what you watch, you are applying the principle of appropriateness well. Everyone inhales the air of the environment they are in, the scent of the flower they smell. Then, you become that flower itself...

WHAT IS THE REAL MESSAGE OF SOMEONE HASSLING YOU?

If someone is hassling you, not all the issues they're dealing with are about you. They are dealing with their own disappointments and projecting them onto you. Perhaps you triggered them with some behavior or words of yours. They might be trying to suppress their own inadequacies through you. Often, they are not even aware of this themselves.

Healed individuals do not take on the disappointments and problems of others, do not blame themselves because of that person, and know how to keep themselves away from this situation. Because they know that the situation has nothing to do with them.

But if you are experiencing an annoying situation with a person, maybe there are some questions you need to ask yourself: What emotion led me to encounter this person? Does this person have a life lesson for me? Is there a message for me in this situation? Asking yourself the right questions leads to finding the right answers.

Perhaps that person is confronting you with a feeling of hurt that you have not dealt with in the past. Because you have a similar feeling, that person has made you a mirror of it. So don't take it personal, but see what is hidden in yourself. You may not be about what that person is experiencing today, but you may be about a feeling from the past.

Once you find that feeling, the healing begins. If we start to look at the people around us as teachers, we also understand that we did not meet them by chance. Life challenges us to teach us something. Sometimes with people we do not know, sometimes with our loved ones. Life does not torment us. It challenges us with people, shows ourselves with traumas, and heals us with illnesses. All of these bring us to balance. Because chaos is necessary before order. So, whenever you experience chaos, know that you will soon put yourself in order."

IS HUMAN ONLY ROOTED IN THE WORLD?

During a period when I was contemplating issues of rooting in the world, I had a dream of a tree hovering above the rocks. I thought a lot about it. The message was this: Human beings root themselves in the earth and in the sky. Human beings also root themselves in each other. With their bodies, souls, and emotions, human beings root themselves everywhere. Sometimes you don't need soil to root or grow roots. You can root and grow roots without soil. Just know how to do it...

Some people root themselves in this life with their children. Some root themselves in their work, their career. Some through helping others, some through socializing, some through solitude... For some, adversity is necessary to root. For others, it is wealth. Since we were born into this world, our needs for rooting have always been different. That's why we live different lives. Those who compare their lives to others are the ones who slow down the pace of evolution. That's why their rooting process takes longer. While they are busy with other lives, they postpone the tasks of their own lives unknowingly.

That's why no one is superior to anyone else. Islam says, 'Superiority is in righteousness,' referring to this understanding and consciousness. The righteous are those who raise their consciousness. To raise one's consciousness, one must devote oneself to one's own spiritual development.

So why do we need to root ourselves in the world?

Because fundamentally, our duty is to understand the lessons of this temporary simulated worldly life and to honor this magnificently designed world. You came to this temporary realm to recognize yourself, the world, and your soul, and to elevate your rank.

Remember, souls came to this world by their own request. And each soul that can evolve with experiences and hardships that meet its needs reaches unity beyond the hereafter and paradise. In the infinite realm it came to, it gathers all its parts together and returns to the essence.

So, what are the things that grow your roots in this life? What subjects ground you and prevent you from flying before completing your tasks? Without knowing this, people cannot appreciate what they experience and have.

ARE YOU SEARCHING FOR YOUR PATH?

If you are going to embark on a journey, first you must know yourself. The destination varies for everyone according to their temperament, soul, and needs. Not everyone can find what they are looking for on the same path. Walking on the path like a Dervish may suit some, being a cavalryman on horseback may suit others, and waiting for a bus on the school road may suit yet another. That's why *Bediuzzaman said, "Do not say, 'My path is the only right path,' say, 'My path is also right.'"

If you ask how you will find your way? Keep asking, the answers to the right questions will come. Some answers come on the wing of a bird, some in your dreams, and some come knocking on your door.

Then you must enter a purification process. You must rid yourself of those who distance you from yourself, those who disturb your soul balance, those who make you feel the need for approval, and those who want to show and be seen. You must also purify your home. Get rid of all excess belongings, those that do not serve you, those that are idle, so that those who serve you and are useful in your life can come in their place.

A little loneliness is good for those who wish to embark on the journey. Do not be sad that you have no friends; you are actually your best friend. The thoughts you used to escape from, the past memories, the traumas, all come back to you, but they have come to say, "Do not run away from us, face us, heal. Then your life will also heal."

Then read and listen only to those who inspire you. Stay away from news that brings your morale down, from social media accounts. Eliminate one by one the social environment and friends that lower your morale. If you do not eliminate, the system will eliminate forcefully, be aware of that. Because if you want to embark on a journey, first the useless energies will be taken away from you. So be willing to let go of everything.

If you find yourself alone, spoil yourself a little. Buy yourself flowers, take nature walks, listen to music, do yoga, dance, knit, pray... Do whatever makes you feel good. All of these will help you connect with your true self.

In this way, you will begin to know yourself, to see the potential within you. You will watch the new you with wonder, and the allure of change and transformation will envelop your soul. You will say, "Thank goodness I embarked on this journey. Because one who knows oneself, knows their Lord."

*Bediuzzaman was a Kurdish Islamic modernist who founded the nondenominational Nur Movement, which advocated for a reinterpretation of Islam according to the needs of a modern society. (https://rpl.hds.harvard.edu/faq/said-nursi)

WHAT IS SPIRITUAL EQUILIBRIUM?

In a state of spiritual equilibrium, a person becomes neutral.

They are free from the need to know, prove, seek approval, be right, or blame.

They are not affected by the positive or negative influences of the outside world.

Instead of blaming someone, they look at life and what they encounter as "What is the message for me in this situation?"

They experience the peace of saying "I am a means" instead of "I did it."

And within this state, they move beyond saying "I am here, I have this" to truly feeling and starting to say "I am not here, there is unity/wholeness."

Because they understand that everyone is a reflection of themselves, that everyone is actually them.

At that point, you are both the one who dies and the one who watches the death. You are both the witness and the one who watches the witness.

You are both immortal and mortal.

You are both the whole universe and nothing.

You are both everything and nothing.

That point is the simplest place you can be.

At that moment, you can make all the readings of life with a single influence, with a single word.

Because that place is beyond knowing, where all confusion ends.

You are in balance.

This state may not always be maintained.

But once you reach it, you are there many times.

So don't tire of trying, of knocking on the door, keep going...

www.ingramcontent.com/pod-product-compliance
Lightning Source LLC
Chambersburg PA
CBHW030222170426
43194CB00007BA/828